DEDICATION

In loving memory of those whose lives shaped mine...
To my beloved parents, Om Prakash and Sheela,
And my parents-in-law, B.D. Mehta and Sita Rani
With sincere gratitude, enduring respect, and eternal love.

RESTLESS ROOTS

How to lead with conviction when your path demands with reinvention

ANIL BHOLLA

Second Edition: February 2026
Printed in India

Printed at: Parksons Graphics

Typeset in EB Garamond

ISBN: 978-93-6070-970-9

Cover Design: Prajakta Sawant

STORYMIRROR
Stories that reflect you

Publisher: StoryMirror Infotech Pvt. Ltd.
Unit No-F/705, 7th Floor, Kailas Corporate Lounge,
Veer Savarkar Road, Vikhroli Park Site,
Vikhroli West, Mumbai-400079,
Maharashtra, India.

Web: storymirror.com
Facebook: @storymirror
Twitter: @story_mirror
Instagram: @storymirror
Email: marketing@storymirror.com

ACKNOWLEDGEMENT

As I reflect on the journey captured within these pages, I am filled with deep gratitude for those who have walked beside me, shaped my thoughts, and supported me in countless ways.

To my parents, Om Prakash and Sheela—You were my first and finest teachers.

To my father, a proud Air Force officer, who lived by the principles of duty, discipline, and honor. Your life was a testament to courage under fire, and composure in the face of adversity. You taught me that true leadership is forged in responsibility and that integrity is non-negotiable.

To my mother, the quintessential officer's wife—resilient, gracious, and endlessly supportive. You created warmth wherever the Air Force took us, embodying strength in transition and grace in uncertainty. Through your quiet sacrifices and unshakable presence, I learned the power of perseverance and compassion.

Together, you gave me the foundation on which every chapter of my life has been built.

To my wife, Anju—your steadfast support has been the anchor of my life, grounding me through every challenge and triumph.

To my daughter, Nidhi, and my son, Rohan—you inspire me every day with your spirit, resilience, and dreams.

To my revered parents-in-law, B.D. Mehta (Bauji) and Sita Rani—

To Bauji, whose love for learning and relentless curiosity inspired me to challenge myself and keep evolving. And to mother-in-law , whose kindness, wisdom, and quiet strength brought comfort and balance to our lives.

To BK Sharma and Pushpa—your love, fortitude, and encouragement continue to guide me, even in your absence.

To Anish and Srishti, thank you for becoming integral members of our family and bringing warmth and joy into our lives.

A special thanks to Nitin Maheshwari, whose faith kindled the spark that gave life to this memoir. Your belief transformed intention into motion,

To Yadunath, whose careful observations and wise counsel have been essential to this book's unfolding.

In appreciation of Sandeep Nair, whose patient encouragement and enduring support have eased every step of this path.

Lastly, to Rajiv Sharma and Sachin Nigam—whose steady presence and inspiring spirit lit the road ahead and brought warmth to every step of this journey.

FOREWORD

Friendships have a way of revealing the essence of a person, and my friendship with Anil Bholla is no exception. We met as classmates and quickly became dear friends, but over the years, I have come to see him as much more: a person of profound character, unshakable perseverance, and endless curiosity. It's these qualities that shine through in his memoir, ***Restless Roots.***

This book isn't just a collection of milestones or achievements; it's a heartfelt journey through the defining moments of Anil's life. From his childhood as an Air Force kid, where the seeds of discipline and adaptability were first sown, to the halls of the Indian Military Academy, where he faced life-changing decisions, Anil has always been unafraid to embrace transformation. His transition into a remarkable 28-year career at HSBC, followed by his global adventures in Botswana and Mauritius, and finally his meaningful pivot into coaching, reflects not just ambition but a deep understanding of life's evolving purpose.

What sets *Restless Roots* apart is its relatability. Through anecdotes that are sometimes poignant, often humorous, and always insightful, Anil brings his experiences to life. Whether navigating the complexities of corporate leadership, immersing himself in diverse cultures, or reflecting on personal relationships, his stories resonate with universal themes: growth, courage, and the ability to adapt to change.

This memoir is more than a recounting of events; it's a guide for anyone facing life's uncertainties. Anil weaves his reflections with practical wisdom, offering readers a map for navigating their own challenges. His candidness, humility, and ability to find meaning in every situation are inspiring, reminding us that every obstacle is an opportunity to grow.

On a personal note, I've had the privilege of seeing Anil's journey unfold over the years, and this book captures his spirit perfectly. It's thoughtful yet approachable, reflective yet forward-looking. It's the story of a man who has embraced every phase of his life with open arms and an open mind. For me, ***Restless Roots*** is a window into Anil's mind and heart. It's a chronicle of a life lived with intention, curiosity, and unwavering optimism.

It's also a reminder that no matter where life takes us, it's the lessons we learn, the people we meet, and the mindset we cultivate that truly define our journey.

As you delve into these pages, you'll find yourself not only learning from Anil's experiences but also reflecting on your own. That's the magic of this book—it doesn't just tell a story; it starts a conversation with the reader.

Anil, my friend, you've written something truly special. It's a testament to your resilience, your wisdom, and your generosity in sharing your life's lessons. To the reader, I can only say this: prepare to be inspired, enlightened, and reminded of the power of perseverance and self-discovery.

Lt Gen YK Joshi (Retd)
PVSM, UYSM, AVSM, VrC, SM

FOREWORD

It is with great pleasure that I write this foreword for Anil Bholla's Restless Roots. My connection to Anil—the classmate of my younger brother and a fellow alumnus of Kendriya Vidyalaya, Faridabad—makes this endeavor even more special. Though our journeys have unfolded across different times and experiences, our shared background creates a profound sense of connection that resonates deeply as I immerse myself in his narrative.

Anil's book is not merely a recounting of events, but a deeply personal reflection on a life lived fully. He generously shares his journey, the highs and lows, the triumphs and setbacks, with an honesty that is both refreshing and inspiring. From his early days in military cantonments, where the sounds of jet engines mingled with the jingles of childhood, to his distinguished career spanning diverse industries and geographical boundaries, Anil paints a vivid picture of a life shaped by experience, resilience, and a constant pursuit of growth.

Anil's narrative also underscores the profound impact of mentors and role models. He acknowledges the guidance he received from others and emphasizes the importance of paying it forward by mentoring aspiring leaders. His transition into coaching, a field where he now empowers individuals to unlock their potential, feels like a natural progression, a testament to his commitment to personal growth and the development of others.

What stands out most in Anil's story is the seamless interplay between his personal and professional life. He eloquently illustrates how lessons from one sphere enrich and inform the other. The discipline instilled during his formative years in a military environment, the adaptability shaped by frequent relocations, and the deep value of relationships cultivated along the way—all come together to form a rich tapestry of experience. Anil does not shy away from challenges, including professional setbacks; instead, he embraces them as opportunities for growth, underscoring the power of perseverance and self-reflection.

Restless Roots is more than just a memoir; it's a guide for navigating the complexities of life. Anil's insights on leadership, the importance of values, and the courage to embrace change will resonate with readers at all stages of their careers. He reminds us that success is not a destination but a continuous journey of learning, adapting, and striving to reach beyond our perceived limitations. I am confident that this book will inspire readers to reflect on their own journeys, embrace their challenges, and pursue their dreams with renewed vigour. I wholeheartedly recommend Restless Roots to anyone seeking inspiration, guidance, and a deeper understanding of the interconnectedness of personal and professional success.

Air Marshal Raghunath Nambiar (Retd)

PVSM, AVSM, VM(G) & Bar

FOREWORD

Like Anil, I too was what was colloquially known as "an Army brat" and to this day look on it with pride - as a badge of Honour. It is a legacy of discipline, honour, and service passed down from our parents—individuals who led with courage, lived with purpose, And when I meet other "brats," I note their pride in something which was not so much taught to them, but which they were born into. Life in the Defence forces is not about what you want but what your country wants and expects from you without questioning. It is a disciplining of one's life which calls for service to others rather than yourself - which is what the best leadership is all about.

Restless Roots is a nostalgic and affirming experience. Anil beautifully captures the spirit of our shared beginnings— of little towns, manicured lawns, the sound of birds and the sight of foxes scurrying to their lairs in the garden of old bungalows we lived in. But above all, the discipline and the camaraderie that accompanied it- and the bugles that told you what time it was and what next was expected of you. These early influences form the foundation of Anil's reflections on leadership and resilience throughout the book.

But this is more than a story of the past. Anil's insights on navigating change, adapting across industries, and leading with integrity come at a time when the world is being reshaped by uncertainty and complexity. As nations and individuals grapple with multipolarity and shifting paradigms, leadership that is rooted in purpose and shaped by experience—like Anil's—is not only relevant, but essential.

It is a privilege to have been asked to write this foreword for someone I worked alongside with over many years. *Restless Roots* is a thoughtful, sincere, and valuable guide for anyone seeking to lead with courage, stay grounded in their values, and rise to the challenges of a rapidly evolving world.

Zarir J Cama

Former HSBC Group General Manager; CEO, HSBC India & Malaysia

PROLOGUE

"You can't really know where you are going until you know where you have been."

— Maya Angelou

It was a quiet January morning in 2024. I sat alone in my home office, reflecting—not on my next big career move, but on everything that had brought me to this point. After decades in leadership roles across countries and industries, I realized that my next chapter wouldn't be about climbing higher. It would be about looking deeper—asking what truly matters, and how I could give back.

That's what this book is about.

It's not a roadmap or a set of rules. It's a collection of real experiences—some tough, some inspiring—that taught me lessons about leadership, success, failure, and growth. My hope is that by sharing these reflections, I can help you—whether you're stepping into your first job, launching a startup, or figuring out what kind of leader you want to become.

Where It All Began

I grew up in military cantonments, where life was defined by structure, community, and resilience. We moved often, so I learned early how to adapt, make new friends, and find stability in change. These early lessons shaped the way I approached both people and problems—and later became the backbone of my leadership style.

As I moved into the corporate world, starting in banking roles across different cities in India, I was exposed to diverse teams, cultures, and working styles. Every new role added something to my understanding—not just about business, but about people and how they grow.

The Corporate Climb

Over four decades, I held senior roles in global companies—including as the COO of a leading bank in Mauritius. I led teams through challenging economic periods, organizational change, and moments of uncertainty. I learned that leadership isn't about knowing all the answers—it's about staying calm when others can't, building trust, and helping people perform at their best.

But success doesn't come in a straight line. There were delays in promotions, changes in leadership, and times when things didn't go the way I expected. Those moments taught me patience, humility, and the power of resilience. Looking back, the setbacks taught me more than the wins ever could.

Mentors Matter

Throughout my career, I had mentors who offered guidance, encouragement, and sometimes tough feedback. Their support helped me stay grounded and focused. Over time, I started mentoring others, and I discovered how powerful it is to help someone else grow. If there's one thing I'd urge you to do—early in your career—it's to seek out mentors. And one day, become one.

What I've Learned About Success

Success isn't just about job titles or paychecks. It's about knowing who you are and staying true to it—even when things get tough. The habits and values I picked up as a child—like discipline, empathy, and curiosity—became the foundation for everything I achieved later.

Your personal and professional lives are not separate. Who you are at home shows up at work. And the person you become in your career influences how you show up in your relationships. The earlier you understand this, the more balanced and meaningful your journey will be.

From Executive to Coach: A Journey of Relearning and Growth

"The best leaders are those who help others lead themselves."

After leaving Mauritius, I found myself at a crossroads. I had decades of experience in leadership, business, and finance—but deep down, I felt the urge to do something more meaningful. My curiosity had long extended beyond strategy and spreadsheets. I was drawn to human behavior, emotional intelligence, and personal growth—the "why" behind what drives people and teams.

It was during a birthday call with a close friend, Rajagopalan (RSR), that the spark ignited. As we spoke about our respective journeys, he casually said, "Why don't you consider becoming a coach?" That question stayed with me. Coaching seemed to unite everything I cared about: leadership, learning, and helping others grow.

I began training under Sharmi Roy, Founder-Director of Art To Lead - Coachezzy, whose mentorship introduced me not just to the tools of coaching, but to its deeper essence. I learned that coaching isn't about telling people what to do—it's about asking the right questions, listening deeply, and creating a safe space for others to discover their own solutions.

Driven by this new purpose, I went through the rigorous certification process guided by the International Coaching Federation (ICF). It wasn't just a professional requirement—it was a transformative experience. I had to unlearn old habits, relearn with intention, and absorb new ways of thinking and being. It was humbling, challenging, and energizing all at once.

In parallel, I earned a Diploma in Modern Applied Psychology, which further enriched my understanding of human behavior and mental frameworks. Everything I had explored—mindfulness, leadership, emotional intelligence, and behavior therapy—now converged through the lens of coaching.

Today, I see coaching not as a job, but as a mission. It allows me to blend decades of global experience with a passion for helping others thrive. And for young professionals stepping into leadership, entrepreneurship, or uncertain paths, I believe coaching can be a powerful catalyst for self-awareness, confidence, and transformation

Why I Wrote This Book

This book is for you—the dreamer stepping into your first office, the young entrepreneur navigating uncertainty, the team lead figuring out how to manage people. I want to share stories and lessons that can help you avoid common mistakes, find your own voice, and lead with clarity and courage.

I've made bold decisions, faced tough setbacks, and reinvented myself more than once. And I'm still learning. But through it all, a few truths have stayed constant:

- **Character matters more than charisma.**
- **Growth comes from discomfort.**
- **Your roots—your values—will carry you through any storm.**

A Final Thought

As you read on, I invite you to reflect—not just on what you want to achieve, but on why. What kind of impact do you want to make? What legacy do you want to build—not years from now, but today?

Because this isn't just a book about my journey. It's a book about yours.

So ask yourself:

What experiences have shaped who you are?

What values do you want to live by?

What risks are worth taking?

And most importantly—what are your *restless roots* calling you toward?

CONTENTS

01

THE FOUNDATIONS OF CHARACTER

CHAPTER 1

Where the Roar of Jet Engines Meets the Hum of Childhood

I was born in Ambala, a city nestled in the heart of Haryana, where the life I knew was shaped by the thrum of jet engines. My father, a proud officer in the Indian Air Force, served in a world that was a blend of discipline, honor, and the ever-present hum of military routine. From the moment I took my first breath, I was immersed in the world of cantonments—enclaves that served as the heart of military life. For us, it wasn't just a home; it was a universe of its own, a microcosm of India, complete with its own set of rules, rhythms, and routines.

Cantonment life was always bustling, with the constant sound of boots marching in unison, salutes exchanged, and the whir of aircraft taking off and landing. It was a life in which time seemed to be measured in military drills and the strict orderliness of the barracks. For someone like me, though, it was an incredibly fascinating environment. While other children spent their time playing traditional games, I spent countless hours watching the planes take off and wondering where they would go. There was always a sense of anticipation, as though the world beyond the cantonment walls was just waiting for us to explore it.

Growing up in an Air Force family meant constant movement. My father's career required frequent relocations, so we packed up and moved to a new city every couple of years. Seven cities in total during my school years. Each move was a mini-adventure, each one forcing me to adapt to a new environment.

Different neighborhoods, new friends, shifting languages, unfamiliar foods, and climates that ranged from the cool air of mesmerizing Srinagar to the oppressive heat of Agra—it was a perpetual cycle of change. We were forever embracing the unknown, learning new ways to live, to communicate, and to fit in.

These constant relocations gave me the chance to witness the changing landscapes of India, from its serene valleys to its hinterland. I was immersed in the contrasts that the country had to offer, and those early years shaped my identity in ways that would carry through to adulthood. In each new location, I became a traveler in my own country, learning to find my place within a different cultural context, yet always holding on to the roots of military life.

Summer vacations were the highlight of the year. We would take long train journeys to our grandparents' home. These journeys were an adventure in themselves, with steam engines chugging along, smudging our faces with coal soot as we stuck our heads out of the windows. My grandfather, a doctor, was both a source of comfort and fear. A slight sneeze, and we would find ourselves bracing for his inevitable injections, delivered with a combination of precision and grandfatherly love.

Reading became my favorite pastime during those summers. My siblings and I would spend hours poring over the family atlas, imagining journeys to distant lands. Collecting stamps and flags became our prized hobbies, fueling a sense of connection to a world that seemed both vast and within reach.

Cantonment Life: Unity in Diversity, with Every Hello and Goodbye

Life in the cantonments was unique—an insulated world filled with vibrant diversity, yet cocooned from the outside. The military life offered its own brand of safety, and for a child, that was comforting. At the same time, it was also a world that exposed us to a melting pot of cultures. My school, the Kendriya Vidyalayas, wasn't just a place to learn, it was the epitome of "unity in diversity" that was not merely a phrase, but a lived experience. In those classrooms, my friends came from every corner of India, each bringing their unique backgrounds with them.

I still remember the first time I made friends with a boy from Tamil Nadu. I had no idea what Idlis or Gunpowder even were, let alone how they tasted. His tiffin box smelled so different from mine—so distinctly southern. We spent hours sharing lunch, me learning about his culture, and him learning about mine. In another cantonment, I befriended a classmate whose family hailed from Bengal, and I was introduced to the world of mustard oil, macher jhol, and the distinct aroma of fish. The food was always a telling sign of the cultures we encountered, and every meal shared was a bridge that connected us across geographical divides.

In one breath, I would be sharing a tiffin with a classmate whose lunchbox smelled of idlis dipped in gunpowder; in the next, I'd be debating the merits of mustard oil in bitter gourd fries with another friend. The diversity was overwhelming at times, but it also taught me to adapt quickly and embrace differences. With every new transfer came new faces, new friends, and new challenges. But perhaps the hardest part was the goodbye—every time we left, we knew that it meant leaving behind not just friends, but whole parts of our identity. However, in this cycle of hellos and goodbyes, we learned resilience. Friendships, though fleeting, were deep and sincere, because we knew that our time together was limited. In that very brevity, there was something so pure about those connections.

But amidst the fleeting friendships, one truth remained constant—the diversity of India was always on display, and I grew to understand and appreciate the vast array of cultural nuances that shaped the nation. Celebrating festivals like Holi, Diwali, and Ganesh Chaturthi was a testament to our community's rich tapestry. Each celebration was a vivid display of colors, laughter, and shared joy, reinforcing the bonds we held as a collective. In our schools, we weren't just learning subjects; we were learning the language of empathy, of connection, and of adaptation. And it was these very skills that would stay with me long after I had moved on to other places.

A Spy, a Chase, and a Child's Wonder

The war had not begun, but tension was palpable. My father was posted at Adampur, a quiet small town between Hoshiarpur and Jalandhar, in Punjab, that was home to one of India's air force bases. It was a world of contrasts. Inside the cantonment, life was organized and secure, with neat rows of houses, well-kept gardens, and disciplined routines. Outside, the chaos of a small town unfolded: crowded bazaars, the aroma of spices, and shops buzzing with activity.

There was a temple which has entrance from two sides in two lanes of shops. Among these shops, one stood out—a modest block-printing shop run by a young man, perhaps in his late twenties. It was a favorite haunt for women, who visited to get their bed sheets and sarees block-printed with intricate designs. The young man seemed harmless, almost endearing, with his shy demeanor and gentle smile. My mother and I often passed by the shop on our trips to the market, marveling at the vibrant patterns displayed outside.

One sunny afternoon, my mother and I decided to step out of the cantonment for some shopping. The market was alive with chatter, haggling, and the clinking of bicycle bells. As we walked past the block printer's shop, a sudden commotion caught our attention. A jeep from the Air Force Police screeched to a halt near the temple, its presence disrupting the humdrum of the bazaar.

Three uniformed police officers stepped out; their expressions grim. They entered the block printer's shop without hesitation. The young owner wasn't inside at the time—he had apparently stepped out for an errand. Moments later, he appeared at the corner of the street, carrying a bundle of fabric. But as soon as his eyes fell on the jeep and the policemen inside his shop, something inexplicable happened.

His face drained of color, and without missing a beat, he turned on his heels and began running. He got inside the temple and exited from the other side. The officers spotted him immediately and gave chase, shouting commands to stop. The narrow lanes of Adampur's village market became the stage for a tense pursuit. Shop owners and pedestrians froze mid-action, their attention riveted on the unfolding drama.

I remember watching in stunned silence as the block printer sprinted and vanished. My heart raced with questions. Why was he running? What had he done? Who was he, really? The air force police weren't far behind, and soon reinforcements arrived. The market was cordoned off, and word spread like wildfire: the young block printer was a spy.

Curiosity got the better of me. As the commotion died down and the policemen secured the shop, I found myself inching closer. The officers had left the shop door slightly ajar in their hurry to join the chase. I glanced at my mother, who was busy talking to her neighbor, and slipped inside.

The shop's interior was unremarkable—a typical workspace with stacks of fabric, wooden stamps, and pots of dye. But my gaze was drawn to a door at the back, half-hidden behind a curtain. Unable to resist, I stepped through it and into a small room.

What I saw made my breath catch. The walls were lined with strange gadgets and wires, blinking lights, and what looked like an array of transmitters. It was like stepping into a different world, one that didn't belong in this quaint shop.

At that moment, I heard a commotion outside and quickly slipped out of the shop. The officers had caught the block printer near the bus stand, where he had tried to board a bus to escape. He was handcuffed and brought back to shop, his face a mask of defeat. The crowd had swelled, and whispers of espionage filled the air. He was then whisked away in the jeep.

That evening, I couldn't stop thinking about what had happened. Over dinner, I turned to my father, an officer in the Air Force, with a flood of questions.

"Why did the block printer run? Was he really a spy? What will happen to him now?"

My father, a calm and composed man, set down his glass of water and met my curious gaze. "Sometimes," he began, "enemies find ways to infiltrate even the safest places. They gather information that can be harmful to the nation. That's why we must always stay vigilant, especially in places like this cantonment."

"But he didn't look like a spy," I protested. "He was just a block printer!"

My father smiled faintly. "Spies rarely look like what you imagine. They blend in, make friends, and build trust. That's what makes them dangerous."

"Will they let him go?" I asked, still grappling with the idea that someone so ordinary could be involved in something so sinister.

"No," my father said firmly. "He'll face a proper investigation. If he's guilty, he'll be punished. This is about the safety of thousands of people, not just the cantonment, but the entire country."

His words stayed with me. For the first time, I realized that the security and peace we enjoyed came at a cost. It wasn't just about soldiers and airplanes, it was about constant vigilance, unseen battles, and the sacrifices made by countless individuals to protect the nation.

Years later, as I think back to that day in Adampur, I can still see the block printer's face, a mix of fear and defiance as he was led away. I often wonder what drove him to become a spy. Was it ideology, coercion, or desperation? I'll never know.

But that incident taught me two invaluable lessons.

First, appearances can be deceiving. The most unassuming person could be harboring the deepest secrets. It's a reminder to stay observant and never take things at face value.

Second, the importance of integrity. The block printer may have been skilled at his craft, but he used his talents for betrayal. Whatever you choose to do in life, do it with honesty and a sense of responsibility, because trust, once broken, is almost impossible to rebuild.

For the young boy I was back then, that day marked the end of innocence. The world wasn't just black and white anymore; it was full of shades of gray, where even a simple block printer could be a player in a high-stakes game of espionage.

War Through the Eyes of a Child: Lessons in Resilience Amidst the Roar of Conflict

In 1971, I experienced something that marked my childhood forever: the Indo-Pak war. At nine years old, I was just beginning to make sense of the world around me when suddenly, everything changed. The sky, once calm and blue, was now filled with the deafening sound of aircrafts taking off, the unmistakable roar of fighter jets becoming part of the daily backdrop. I could identify their engines with ease, the same way a birdwatcher might recognize a particular bird call. But this wasn't a hobby; this was a matter of survival.

The war was an experience that no child should have to endure, yet for those of us who grew up in cantonments, it became a part of our reality. Nights were spent huddled in trenches as the world outside seemed to explode in a cacophony of sound. The air was thick with tension, and the sky glowed with the streaks of anti-aircraft fire. I remember the fear that hung in the air, not just from the bombings but from the uncertainty of it all. What made this period even more poignant, though, was not the dramatic moments of war but the quiet courage of my mother. She was a pillar of strength, never once letting her own fear show. While children like me tried to make light of the situation, hiding our fears behind games and stories, my mother bore the weight of worry in silence. She was the unspoken anchor, holding everything together, teaching me the true meaning of courage without uttering a word.

In hindsight, those nights in the trenches were as much about waiting and wondering as they were about survival. The sound of jets overhead became a constant companion, and the blackouts, the drills, and the whisper of worried conversations between the adults around us painted a vivid picture of the conflict. Yet, despite it all, life continued. The stories my mother would tell us in hushed tones, trying to distract us from the sounds of war outside, were my first lessons in resilience.

Srinagar: In the Valley of Contradictions, Where Beauty Meets Bewilderment

After the war, we moved to Srinagar in 1972. The Kashmir Valley was a place of unmatched beauty, with its pristine lakes, towering mountains, and lush gardens. But beneath this natural splendor, there was an undercurrent of unrest that I could feel even as a child. It was a place of contradictions, where the serenity of the landscape often belied, the tensions simmering beneath the surface.

School in Srinagar was a mix of the usual joys and challenges, but there was something unique about the place. It wasn't just the landscape that fascinated me; it was the people and their stories. Some of my classmates, local children from non-military background, would often speak in ways that puzzled me. "This is from your India," they would say with a tone that implied a separation. I didn't understand it at the time, but looking back, I realize that their words reflected the complex political realities of the region.

Despite the unease that loomed over the city, my memories of Srinagar are more tied to the stories I heard from the seniors in school. They spoke of heroics—of dogfights between aircraft and the bravery of soldiers. Names like Flt Lt Nirmal Jit Singh

Sekhon, 2nd Lt Arun Khetrapal, Lance Naik Albert Ekka, Field Marshal Sam Manekshaw became more than just words; they were part of the fabric of our lives. Yet, to me, these stories were more than just tales of war; they were markers of valor, of people who had faced extraordinary circumstances and risen above them. At that age, I couldn't fully grasp the magnitude of it all, but the idea of bravery and sacrifice stayed with me.

And amidst all the tension and uncertainty, Srinagar's beauty never ceased to amaze me. The Dal Lake, with its calm waters, the shikaras, Nishat and Shalimar Bagh, the Shankaracharya Temple, in the distance, it was a place of contrasts—both peaceful and unsettling at the same time. The best part was a steady stream of relatives visiting us, and we used to be their tour guides, showing them around Gulmarg and Pahalgam, willingly and excitedly.

Agra: From the Mountain Breeze to the Dry Heat

In 1974, we moved to Agra, a city so different from the cool, crisp air of Srinagar that it felt like a world apart. The heat of Agra in the summer was oppressive, and I, still a child, was ill-prepared for the furnace-like heat that would become our reality for the next one year. Yet, there was an adventure in every change—whether it was adjusting to the scorching weather or getting to know a completely different way of life.

It was during this time that I found an escape through comics—primarily, the Commando comics. These stories became my world. I imagined myself as one of those soldiers, battling through jungles and deserts, saving the day, and coming out victorious. Along with my friends, I reenacted these adventures, climbing trees and pretending to parachute into action. Our "missions" were never life-threatening, but in our minds, we were soldiers, taking on the world with every step.

The summers in Agra were long, dry, and intense. The scorching heat was only tempered by the monsoon rains, which arrived with great fanfare, bringing relief to the parched earth. The rainy season felt like a festival, and we would run through the streets, soaking in the first rains with childlike joy. Agra's famous Petha and Dal Moth were staple snacks. Those were the moments I cherished—simple, yet filled with a sense of freedom and connection to the land.

The Life that Shapes You: Of Discipline, Duty, and Dreams of a Larger World

Growing up in a military cantonment was about more than just a physical space; it was about a way of life—a culture rooted in discipline, respect, and a sense of duty. The daily routines of military life provided structure, and within that structure, I found both comfort and confinement. There was something comforting about knowing that every morning would begin with the crisp sound of marching boots and soldiers going about their day with purpose.

My father was the embodiment of those values. He wasn't just a logistics officer; he was a figure of inspiration; someone whose stories of sacrifice and camaraderie shaped my understanding of leadership. I remember the pride I felt when he spoke of his time in the Air Force, stories that were both thrilling and humbling. From him, I learned that leadership isn't about demanding respect; it's about earning it through integrity and compassion.

As a child, I was exposed to a world where competition and camaraderie coexisted. The frequent relocations made me adaptable, while the shared experiences of moving from one cantonment to another fostered a sense of unity among my siblings and me. Despite the differences in each place, we always found solace in one another. Together, we navigated the challenges that came with being military children—challenges that, in hindsight, shaped our character in ways we couldn't fully comprehend then.

Education played a pivotal role in my development. The numerous schools I attended shaped me in different ways. I was exposed to a variety of pedagogies, and each one left its mark. I was fortunate to have some incredible teachers who inspired me to think critically and independently. It wasn't just academics, but also the extracurricular activities that shaped my personality.

Patriotism Woven into the Fabric of Our Lives

Patriotism was an idea I grew up with, but it wasn't taught in the way you might expect. It wasn't about waving flags or chanting slogans—it was about a deep respect for the country's traditions and history. It was about understanding the sacrifices made by the generations before us and feeling a personal responsibility to contribute to the nation's well-being.

In the Air Force, patriotism was woven into the very fabric of our lives. It was a quiet, everyday commitment—a commitment that shaped everything from our work ethic to our interactions with others. I learnt early on that serving others was not just a duty; it was a privilege. Whether it was helping a neighbor or contributing to the community, there was always a sense of service that transcended personal gain. It was the cornerstone of our upbringing.

Bridging the Past with the Future

The life I lived in those formative years, the years spent amidst the roar of jet engines and the quiet wisdom of my parents—shaped me into who I am today. But perhaps the most important lesson I learned was that home is not just a place but the people and the experiences that stay with you. Those years taught me the value of resilience, diversity, and service to something greater than oneself.

As I look back now, with all the lessons I've learned from those early years, I realize that I was not just raised in a military family. I was raised by a country. And the stories of courage, sacrifice, and unity that I grew up with continue to inspire me every day.

CHAPTER 2

Crossroads in Faridabad: A Journey of Transformation

Faridabad was a small industrial town on the outskirts of Delhi, still far from the bustling urban sprawl that would later define the National Capital Region. Faridabad's primary identity was rooted in its industrial growth, which had begun to take shape in the early 1950s. The town, located in Haryana, was home to a number of small and medium-scale factories. These factories were mainly involved in manufacturing items like hosiery, shoes, and machine tools, as well as industries in textiles and automobiles. While Faridabad was still relatively quaint and unassuming compared to its future expansion, it was a town that represented the early days of industrialization in India. It was a place where hard work and simplicity were celebrated, and where the seeds of the modern-day Faridabad were being quietly sown.

In 1975, we moved to Faridabad. It was here in Kendriya Vidyalaya school. that I met Rajiv Sharma, who would become my life's best buddy. I had another classmate, Earnest Aaron, and we shared a dream—to join the Air Force. Together, we spent hours poring over his father's log book, aeronautical trivia, sketching aircraft, and planning our futures as fighter pilots.

Pranks, Punctures, and Perspective: Lessons from Mischief

Class X remains a treasure trove of fond memories, mischief, and musings. Amid all the camaraderie and chaos, there was one boy who stood out—Sanjay aka potato. He was, for lack of a better term, an overachiever. While most of us struggled to simply exist within the confines of academic rigors and adolescent hormones, Sanjay managed to rise above it all. He was tall, chubby and blessed with the aura of someone who had already figured out life.

Sanjay's competitiveness was both inspiring and, well, mildly annoying. Whether it was academics, drawing and painting, or even mundane tasks like organizing classroom supplies, he approached everything with precision. It was no surprise, then, when he was appointed as the class monitor—a role he embraced as if he'd been chosen to protect the nation.

For the uninitiated, being a class monitor meant two things. First, you were tasked with carrying out entire stacks of notebooks to the staff room—something Sanjay managed with ease, unlike the rest of us who treated it as the equivalent of manual labor. Second, and more importantly, you had to maintain discipline in the classroom when the teacher was absent.

Now, you must understand that asking a room full of fifteen-year-olds to sit quietly for more than five minutes is akin to asking a volcano not to erupt. Naturally, the room would descend into a symphony of chatter, laughter, munching on hidden snacks, and the occasional friendly wrestling match. This was where Sanjay's unwavering sense of duty came into play. Armed with chalk and an iron will, he would stride up to the blackboard and begin writing the names of troublemakers.

"Sunil Manchanda. Talking."

"Rajeev. Eating in class."

"Anil. Laughing too loudly."

It was like the roll call of doom. As soon as the teacher returned, Sanjay would read out his list of offenders with the solemnity of a court marshal. Predictably, punishments were meted out with great affection. They ranged from standing on the bench to holding one's ears and hands above head. My personal favorite was being sent outside the class to stand like a scarecrow, a punishment that allowed us to enjoy a mild breeze and chat with fellow "scarecrows."

But here's where the story takes a turn. Sanjay's dedication to law and order did not sit well with us. To us, he wasn't just a disciplinarian; he was a snitch, an informant, and a perpetual thorn in the side of youthful rebellion. Something had to be done.

The Great Puncture Plot

Our plan was born during one particularly long lunch break. As we munched on our aloo parathas and idols, we hatched a scheme that, in hindsight, was both ingenious and slightly malicious. The weapon of choice? The humble divider from our geometry box. The target? Sanjay's beloved bicycle.

Our school had a sprawling cycle stand where scores of bicycles stood in neat rows. Sanjay's cycle, of course, was easy to spot. It was the one with the shiny Atlas with green frame and perfectly aligned handlebars, a reflection of its owner's meticulous personality.

The plan was simple. As soon as we were punished and sent outside the class (which, let's face it, was inevitable), we would ask the teacher for permission to use the restroom. With divider in hand, we would make our way to the cycle stand, locate Sanjay's bike, and surreptitiously poke tiny holes in the tyre.

The execution of the plan was nothing short of cinematic. On one such day, I found myself outside the classroom, holding my ears as a form of penance for laughing too loudly. As soon as the teacher's back was turned, I made my move. With the divider tucked in my pocket, I sprinted to the cycle stand, my heart pounding with a mix of fear and exhilaration.

Finding Sanjay's bike, I crouched down and carefully punctured the rear tire. The air hissed out in a satisfying whisper, and I felt a strange sense of justice. My accomplice Sunil soon joined me, taking turns to ensure both tires were equally deflated.

When the final bell rang, the cycle stand transformed into a bustling hive of activity. Students grabbed their bicycles and pedaled away, eager to get home. Sanjay, however, stood frozen in disbelief, staring at his deflated tires. Watching him wheel his bicycle to the nearest puncture repair shop felt like sweet revenge. We exchanged gleeful glances, basking in the satisfaction of our rebellion.

It became a regular affair. But our triumph was short-lived. Sanjay's parents met the principal and requested that he be relieved of his monitoring responsibilities.

Looking back, I can't help but feel a mix of amusement and guilt. At the time, we saw Sanjay as the enemy, the embodiment of everything that stood between us and our teenage freedom. Yet, the truth is, he was just doing his job, and doing it well.

I now see Sanjay in a different light.

His discipline, dedication, and sense of responsibility were qualities that most of us lacked at that age. While we were busy poking holes in his tyres, he was quietly building the foundation for a successful future. He took his role as class monitor seriously, even if it made him unpopular. It's a reminder that every role, no matter how small, deserves commitment and respect.

Our mischief, though harmless in hindsight, came from a place of immaturity. Sanjay's maturity and focus stood in stark contrast to our impulsive need for revenge. What seemed like an act of justice to our teenage minds now feels like a childish prank. Time has a way of putting things into perspective, showing us the bigger picture.

The Final Word

Life, in many ways, is like a classroom. It's full of lessons, some taught by teachers, and others learned through our own experiences. Sanjay, in his stoic and disciplined way, taught me that integrity often comes at the cost of popularity.

If I could meet him today, I'd probably apologize for the punctured tires and commend him for being the kind of person we all secretly aspired to be. And who knows? Perhaps, in his own quiet way, Sanjay would forgive me, with the same grace he exhibited all those years ago.

Pedaling Into Adventure, Learning For a Lifetime

The summer of 1977 was an unrelenting stretch of heat and boredom. Our exams were done, and we had all the time in the world, yet no clue what to do with it. Television was non-existent, and our primary sources of entertainment were books, magazines, and the occasional gossip over the balcony. We devoured Reader's Digest, Illustrated Weekly of India, and even Sarita, the Hindi magazine my mother faithfully subscribed to. Novels, too, were our lifeline—Hardy Boys, Enid Blyton, Sherlock Holmes, and the forbidden thrill of Sydney Sheldon and James Hadley Chase.

But books only provided momentary escape. We were restless, itching for something that would shake us out of the monotony.

The First Ride

One blazing morning, Ernest and I decided to simply ride our bicycles and see what's on the other side of old Faridabad across Mathura Road. We were curious where the road would take us. Without a destination, we pedaled straight out of our NIT 4 complex and crossed Mathura Road. It was the kind of freedom that only teenagers could savor—an open road and the wind in our faces.

The journey was an adventure in itself. We cycled through wilderness, past vacant fields, and across narrow drains that seemed to appear out of nowhere. We reached a point when the road ended one point, by a large drain, its murky waters flowing lazily under the hot sun. We stared at it, half in disgust and half in fascination, before turning back toward home.

When we finally returned, tired but satisfied, disaster struck. Both our bikes had punctured tyres.

"What do we tell them?" Ernest asked, panic creeping into his voice.

"We will just say how do we know," I replied confidently.

We got the puncture repaired, spun a convincing story, and escaped any serious questioning. But that little escapade had planted a seed in our minds.

"What if we went on Mathura Road?" Ernest said, his voice dropping to a conspiratorial whisper.

"Like... towards Delhi?" I replied, the idea taking shape in my mind.

We grinned at each other, knowing we had stumbled upon something thrilling.

Mission Delhi

Over the next few days, we quietly prepared for our next adventure. We didn't tell anyone about our plan, partly because we weren't sure we'd go through with it and partly because we knew we'd never get permission.

Then, one morning, we set out.

This time, we had a clear goal: reach Delhi. Mathura Road stretched ahead like an endless promise, and we were determined to conquer it. The first few kilometers were a breeze, our legs fresh and spirits high.

As we left the familiar sights of Faridabad behind, the landscape changed. We passed factories, dusty bus stops, and occasional roadside vendors, each pedal stroke taking us closer to the bustling capital. The wilderness of the earlier ride was replaced by the hum of trucks and buses on the highway.

It was exhilarating and exhausting. By the time we reached Okhla Industrial Estate, a good 20 kilometers from home, the sun was high, and we were drenched in sweat. Our stomachs growled loudly, and our water bottles were long empty.

"I am hungry," Ernest said, his voice a croak.

We spotted a roadside stall selling kulcha-matar(bread and peas). Between us, we had a grand total of 1 rupee and 10 paisa. It wasn't much, but it was enough. Two plates of kulcha-matar cost 50 paise each, leaving just enough for two glasses of chilled water. The food tasted like heaven, and the water was a godsend in the scorching heat.

The Ride Back

The journey back was a different story altogether. The sun, which had been a mild companion in the morning, now blazed down like an angry taskmaster. The thrill of adventure gave way to the painful reality of dehydration and exhaustion. Every push of the pedals felt like torture, and we stopped frequently, searching in vain for shade or water.

By the time we reached home around 1 PM, we were unrecognizable—sunburnt, dripping with sweat, and stumbling like a pair of drunks. We parked our bikes and slipped into our homes, hoping no one would notice the sorry state we were in.

That night, the consequences of our adventure caught up with us. Both Ernest and I came down with severe heatstroke, complete with high fever and pounding headaches. For the next week, we were confined to our beds, sipping ORS and listening to our mothers' lectures about staying indoors during the summer.

But the funniest part? No one knew the real reason behind our condition. Our little escapade remained a closely guarded secret, a mischievous badge of honor shared only between us.

Looking back, that summer adventure was equal parts foolish and memorable. We had no plan, no resources, and no idea what we were getting ourselves into. But we had something far more valuable—the reckless courage of youth and an unshakable sense of curiosity.

That ride taught me many things: the importance of preparation, the dangers of underestimating nature, and the sheer joy of doing something just for the thrill of it. It also left me with a story—a story of two boys, a rickety pair of bicycles, and a secret journey into the unknown.

Sometimes, the best lessons in life come from the most unexpected adventures. And sometimes, the only way to learn them is to hop on a bike, pedal into the wilderness, and see where the road takes you.

Faridabad and the Civilian Awakening

Faridabad, a city far removed from the buzzing Air Force bases I had grown up around, wasn't a cantonment but a central government complex with a modest Air Force establishment tucked away in its midst. For the first time, I found myself mingling with peers who weren't tied to the armed forces. This change shifted my perspective on life, introducing me to a world where ambitions, choices, and life paths were shaped by entirely different circumstances.

Faridabad brought a mix of friendships that enriched my teenage years. My new friends came from diverse backgrounds—some from business families, others from households of government employees. Conversations ranged from local dynamics to tales of career aspirations, a contrast to the discipline-laden chatter of life in the forces.

My classmates were fiercely academic, with a razor-sharp focus on engineering and medicine, fields synonymous with prestige and promise in middle-class India of the 1970s. Many of them had their career paths mapped out, often guided by parents whose ambitions for their children were as precise as a military mission plan.

By the time we reached our board exams, the results were a testament to this focused determination. Nineteen of my classmates went on to join engineering colleges, and a few pursued medicine. Sushil became an architect, crafting buildings where dreams could be housed. But the one name etched in all our memories was Manoj Mittal, who secured the second rank in the All-India CBSE merit list, a feat that had the entire school buzzing.

My school years in Faridabad were some of the most enriching. Yet, life had its way of testing those ambitions. Despite Earnest and me sharing a dream, and both of us having Airforce background, we couldn't clear the NDA (National Defence Academy) entrance exam. We didn't even know that two of our classmates, Yogesh and Hitesh, had made it already.

A New Path for Me

In the midst of this academic fervor, I found myself grappling with a reality I hadn't anticipated: I didn't score enough to join the ranks of engineering aspirants. It wasn't an easy realization, especially when surrounded by friends whose futures seemed firmly anchored. The decision to pursue commerce wasn't a fallback; it was a calculated choice to carve a different path for myself. Earnest by then had moved out to Chandigarh where his father was posted.

At this pivotal moment, my father too got transferred to Tezpur, Assam. However, my father wanted us to stay back in Faridabad, while he moved east. This separation marked a turning point in my understanding of the nomadic life inherent in the armed forces. While I had always been aware of the frequent relocations, staying back in Faridabad gave me a glimpse of what life could be like without the protective cocoon of family constantly around.

Lessons Beyond the Classroom

These years were not just about academics or career decisions. They were a time of learning about the complexities of the civilian world. In Faridabad, I saw how families built their lives on a foundation of long-term stability—a concept alien to me at the time. Our friend's parents often talked about their children starting school and finishing university in the same city, a stark contrast to my own scattered schooling.

At the same time, I realized the richness of my nomadic upbringing. While most of my friends from Faridabad had a relatively fixed set of experiences, I carried with me fragments of Srinagar's valleys, Agra's scorching summers, and Ambala's military buzz. These diverse experiences gave me a sense of adaptability that would prove invaluable in the years to come.

Faridabad also gave me friendships that transcended time. Rajiv Sharma, my best buddy from school, was a brother from another mother, became the kind of friend who didn't need constant updates to remain close. We shared countless hours discussing life, dreams—our conversations seamlessly weaving between reality and fantasy. Similarly, Ajay Sharma, a junior in school, was my residential block buddy.

While Faridabad gave me lifelong bonds, I didn't lose touch with the friends I'd made in Srinagar and Agra. Even now, decades later, there's a shared warmth when we reminisce about those childhood days. It's a reminder that while the armed forces may scatter its families across the country, the ties forged during those years remain remarkably strong.

The years from 1975 to 1982 were a period of growth and introspection. Moving from a strictly military environment to a civilian one gave me a new perspective on life's possibilities. It wasn't just about careers or academics but about understanding people, aspirations, and the societal framework outside the cantonment gates.

Faridabad taught me to appreciate the stability of a civilian life while also cherishing the dynamism of my own upbringing. It was a chapter where friendships deepened, dreams evolved, and the realization dawned that life, much like the Air Force, is filled with unexpected takeoffs and landings.

Looking back, my childhood feels like a patchwork quilt, each transfer adding a unique square to the tapestry. The experiences were diverse, the challenges many, but the lessons were invaluable.

The constant movement may have denied me the rootedness many children experience, but it gave me a broader worldview. Whether it was learning to appreciate the quiet fortitude of my mother during wartime or understanding the weight of my father's responsibilities, these early years instilled values that would guide me through the rest of my life.

And while I may not have become the fighter pilot I once dreamed of being, the boy who spent his nights imagining himself as a comic book hero found his own way to navigate the skies of life—sometimes soaring, sometimes landing hard, but always ready for the next takeoff.

The 7.25 am Shuttle

The 7:25 AM passenger train to New Delhi was more than just a mode of transportation for me. It was a classroom on wheels, a social hub, and occasionally, an amusement park ride. With the unrelenting rhythm of the train's wheels on the tracks, I embarked daily on my journey from Faridabad to PGDAV College, located in South Campus, Delhi. My fellow passengers were mostly students, office-goers, and the odd vendors, each contributing to the cacophony of our mornings. Among this bustling crowd, my partners-in-commute were two of my closest classmates: Ish Kapur and Rakesh Chopra.

We were three musketeers, or perhaps three jesters, depending on the day. Ish was the charming rogue with a Royal Enfield motorcycle that roared like a lion but purred like a cat on Mathura Road. Rakesh was the pragmatic one, loved to enjoy cups of tea at the station kiosk along with crispy bread pakora, and seemed to have a sixth sense for locating the least crowded compartment. And then there was me, the self-proclaimed strategist, whose ideas were occasionally brilliant but mostly led us into trouble.

College Life: A Theatrical Affair

PGDAV was a different world altogether. Known as one of the best commerce colleges in South Campus, it was an ideal mix of academics, gallivanting, and endless opportunities for procrastination. Classes were optional, or at least we treated them as such, and bunking was an art form we had mastered. Our favorite indulgence was morning show movies at nearby cinemas, where an auditorium filled with college students created an atmosphere that rivaled a cricket stadium.

Theatrics didn't end at the cinema. Our escapades were peppered with harmless pranks, exaggerated stories, and running jokes. One particularly memorable afternoon, we bunked an entire day of lectures to catch a newly released blockbuster. Ish, with his usual flair, bought tickets for the front row. By the time we left the theatre, our necks were sore from looking up at the screen, but our spirits were sky-high.

First year was a breeze. Life was an endless loop of laughter, discovery, and occasional panic before exams. But as second year dawned, something clicked. Maybe it was the looming shadow of final year, or perhaps it was just guilt catching up with us, but we all decided to get serious—or as serious as three college students could be.

It was the evening before our final year exams, and I was perched on my first-floor balcony, enjoying the cool breeze. The road below was quiet, except for the occasional scooter sputtering past. Suddenly, the familiar thrum of Ish's Royal Enfield broke the monotony. There he was, grinning ear to ear and waving a piece of paper like it was a treasure map.

Ish screeched to a halt, bounded up the stairs two at a time, and burst into the balcony. "Look at this!" he said, brandishing the paper. "Tomorrow's question paper!"

I couldn't help but laugh. "Stop being a fool, Ish. Go study," I said, waving him off. He tried convincing me, swearing by every god he could think of that it was authentic. I refused to take the bait, sending him off with a half-hearted chuckle.

The next morning, as I sat in the exam hall and flipped over the question paper, my jaw dropped. The questions were an exact match to Ish's "treasure map." Every single one.

By the time I handed in my paper, my mind wasn't on the exam—it was on Ish and his miraculous find. That evening, I tracked him down and demanded he get the next question paper. Ish, ever the enthusiast, promised to deliver.

True to his word, Ish showed up the next evening with another question paper. This time, I didn't scoff. We spent the night diligently preparing every question on that sheet, completely confident we were ahead of the game. Sleep was sacrificed at the altar of preparation, and by dawn, we were practically giddy with anticipation.

The moment of truth arrived as we sat down for the exam. The invigilator handed out the question papers, and I opened mine with a smug grin.

The grin vanished. Not a single question matched. Not one.

I glanced over at Ish, who was already glaring at me as though I had personally written the fake question paper. We spent the rest of the exam in a fog of panic, scribbling whatever half-remembered answers we could muster. By the time the bell rang, we had moved on from shock to disbelief, and finally, to laughter.

The blame game began as soon as we exited the hall. "It was your idea to rely on this!" I accused him.

"You were the one who insisted we stop studying!" Ish shot back. We went back and forth, each argument more ridiculous than the last, until we finally collapsed in fits of laughter. The fiasco became one of our favorite stories, a tale we would recount at reunions, weddings, and even over Zoom calls decades later.

Looking back, that episode was less about exams and more about friendship, trust, and the art of not taking oneself too seriously. College life, with its myriad adventures, was a crucible that forged bonds stronger than any question paper could break.

We all have our 'Ish moments,' don't we? Times when we put our faith in something or someone, only to see it unravel in unexpected ways. But isn't that what makes life interesting? It's the missteps, the laughter, and the lessons learned that color our memories and give them meaning.

As I sit here reflecting on those carefree days, I can't help but wonder: When was the last time you laughed at your own mistakes and cherished them for what they taught you?

CHAPTER 3

The Call of Duty and the Road Less Travelled

Joining the Indian Military Academy (IMA)

Growing up in military cantonments, the idea of joining the armed forces was more than just a career choice; it was a way of life. Our conversations revolved around the valor of soldiers, the power of tanks, the intricacies of aircraft, and the strategic prowess of submarines. Discussions often drifted towards tales of bravery from the front lines, weaving an unbreakable bond between my upbringing and a fervent desire to serve my nation.

This environment fostered a deep-seated respect for the military and a yearning to be part of that esteemed community. The pride of donning a uniform, the camaraderie of service, and the thrill of defending our country became the cornerstones of my identity. Stories shared by relatives who served, alongside the disciplined life in cantonments, instilled a sense of nationalism that was both profound and unwavering.

As I arrived at the Indian Military Academy (IMA), I felt a mixture of excitement and apprehension. The grand architecture of the academy signified the legacy of those who had walked its halls before me. It was a place where dreams took flight, but it was also a crucible that would test my mettle.

The initial days were overwhelming, filled with a barrage of new experiences that challenged my physical endurance and mental resilience. Each morning began with alarm, signaling us to rise and prepare for the rigorous training that lay ahead. Physical training was unrelenting—endless runs, drills, and exercises designed to break us down and build us back up stronger.

I remember one particularly grueling morning during our first month, when we faced the daunting obstacle course, I realized that my experience in military life was only a small fraction of what I was about to endure. The camaraderie built during these challenges was profound; we encouraged each other, lending strength when fatigue threatened to overwhelm us. It was in these moments that I learned the true essence of teamwork, a lesson that would resonate throughout my life.

Mussoorie Night

It was February 5th, a cold Saturday night in Meiktila Company, Thimaya Battalion, at the Indian Military Academy, that would become infamous in our lives as Mussoorie Night.

I was lying down in my cabin, savoring a rare moment of calm, when I heard it—the frantic running and Baiju's unmistakable voice cutting through the chilly air. "Attention, attention, attention, Meiktila Company! Everyone fall in, immediately!" He was bolting from one platoon quadrangle to another, sounding like a broken alarm clock that had gone rogue.

Chaos erupted. I scrambled out, pulling on my gown as shouts and curses flew from all corners. Despite Baiju's dramatic warnings, it took us fifteen minutes just to assemble. Fifteen minutes! Naturally, the seniors were livid.

Ballu, the towering hulk of a senior, exploded. "You lazy bums! Fall in means fall in! Change to PT rig in 5 minutes! GO!"

We sprinted back to our cabins like headless chickens. Five minutes? Not a chance. Ten minutes later, most of us were still fumbling with shoelaces or hunting for our olive jerseys.

When we finally regrouped, the seniors looked ready to explode. Tomar, with his characteristic calm menace, growled, "You've got sixty seconds to change into your birthday rig! Let's see if you can beat the clock, or should we start counting your birthdays here tonight?"

Sixty seconds. That's all they gave us. Shirts, shorts, socks, shoes—everything flew in every direction as we stripped faster than a magic trick. For once, adrenaline made us efficient. We were all back, stark and shivering, just as his watch hit 50 seconds.

"About time you did something right! Now the fun begins," smirked Tomar. We didn't know whether to be relieved or terrified. The answer became clear soon enough.

"Start rolling," barked Ballu. And so, we rolled—front rolls, side rolls, back rolls—until the grass felt like it had transformed into razor blades. My arms were burning, my back screaming, but I dared not stop. Aaypee, ever the philosopher, rolled past me muttering, "This must be what grass feels like when it's mowed."

When the rolling ceased, we were ordered to climb the divider wall. Terror Thapar, the dreaded CSM, was supervising this phase of our punishment. "On the other side is a surprise, GC! Move it!"

Scaling the wall felt like climbing Everest, given our exhaustion. What awaited us on the other side? A gleaming steel barrel filled with water so cold, it seemed to be in competition with

Siberia. "Jump in! One by one! Don't waste time!" snapped Tomar.

The first jump felt like being stabbed by icicles. Aaypee screamed, "Saraon, are we being punished or preserved for future generations?!" Baiju, never one to hold back, added, "I'm telling you; this is how they invented naturopathy!"

When the last of us emerged, teeth chattering, Ballu declared, "Still cold? Don't worry. Cold showers will fix that! To the showers!" If you've never felt the joy of taking an ice-cold shower in the dead of winter, let me spare you—it's unforgettable, for all the wrong reasons.

Drenched and freezing, we were marched back to the open field. "Now, face Mussoorie and draw warmth from its lights," Tomar said with mock sympathy. There we stood, barely clothed, locked in rigid attention, staring at the twinkling hill station in the distance. It felt like Mussoorie was laughing at us.

In the silence, Aaypee whispered, "You know, if this light therapy works, I am going to give it in double dose to our next course." Baiju grumbled back, "Who is going to be here. I'm taking bus to Agra tomorrow.

The ordeal lasted hours but felt like days. By the end of it, we were frozen to the bone but united in spirit. That night, under Mussoorie's mocking lights, we learned a truth no training manual could teach—grit isn't something you find; it's something you earn.

Years later, whenever the memories of Mussoorie Night resurface, I don't dwell on the cold or the punishment. What I remember is the camaraderie, the shared misery, and the indomitable spirit of Meiktila Company. And yes, Baiju's announcements, which still echoes in my ears.

Academic Challenges and Personal Growth

Academically, IMA presented its own set of challenges. The curriculum was demanding, covering subjects that ranged from military strategy to history and leadership. I immersed myself in learning about military tactics, captivated by how battles were won not merely through force, but through careful planning and execution. The more I learned, the more my admiration for military leaders grew.

Life at The Indian Military Academy (IMA) was not solely confined to physical and academic challenges. The social dynamics of the academy were rich and varied. Frequent socials and events allowed cadets from diverse backgrounds to forge bonds, celebrating our differences while sharing the common goal of military service.

IMA is a place where grit, camaraderie, and discipline are forged under immense pressure. My year-long journey at the academy was no different, filled with valuable lessons, life-long friendships, and unforgettable experiences.

Socials are an integral part of any academy. I was fortunate to belong to multiple 'types' of social groups—schoolmates, city friends, and even NDA acquaintances, having stayed in multiple places. It was at IMA that these connections became my safety net.

I vividly remember my first social event, where nerves faded away amidst laughter and conversation. It was a melting pot of personalities, each cadet bringing their own experiences and perspectives. Among my peers was a fellow cadet named Lota, known for his aloof demeanor. Our playful rivalry became a source of amusement, as every interaction was marked by teasing and laughter. Today, we share fond memories of our time at IMA, often reflecting on how those early interactions forged lasting friendships.

During academy socials and outdoor activities, I often ran into old classmates.

Earnest Aaron

I distinctly recall meeting three from my Faridabad days, including Earnest, who was a course senior. Earnest went on to join the Artillery and later fulfilled his dream of becoming a helicopter pilot. Tragically, fate intervened, and we lost him in a crash three years into his service.

RIP, Earnest—you lived and died a hero.

Reunion with Kulwant

One evening, our battalion commander, lovingly referred to as 'Betty,' asked, "Where is Lota?" The name instantly took me back to my most well dressed and stylist buddy from KV Srinagar. I was eager to reconnect, but Lota was unwell and hospitalized. A few days later, I spotted a smart Sikh gentleman with nameplate tab that read "KS Lota." Excited, I approached him, saying, "Hi, Kulwant!" To my surprise, he coldly rebuffed me with a blunt "FO" and walked away. I learned that at the IMA, seniority mattered, and familiarity from the past could wait.

Years later, in 2010, I received a Facebook message from none other than Lota. He wanted to confirm if I was the Anil Bholla from KV Srinagar. When we finally met, Lota not only remembered the incident but also apologized profusely for his behavior. Today, both of us are in Mumbai, and every time we meet, he jokingly brings up that day, and apologizes!

The Night Watch

We had a senior from NDA who was my next-door neighbor. For reasons unknown, he came under scrutiny, and we were tasked to keep a watch on him all night, with each of us taking hourly shifts. It felt surreal standing guard outside his cabin. But the next morning brought a twist: he casually strolled up from outside, asking why I was loitering by his door! That was my first facepalm moment at the academy.

The Price of Liberty

Liberty days were a precious escape from the grind of the academy. On one such trip to Dehradun, I was caught by a Directing Staff (DS) admiring a beautiful lady in the market. He smirked and said, "Enough of seeing—now come and see me at 8 PM." What followed was a memorable punishment. For weeks, every time this DS saw me, I had to start front-rolling on the spot. Post-lunch, he'd stand outside his office, waiting to catch me, ensuring I perfected my "rolling" technique. I almost stopped looking at beautiful ladies.

The Haircut Disaster

Mandatory haircuts were a weekly ritual, but one Sunday, I missed it after visiting a relative. My buddy and I decided to take matters into our own hands. Armed with razors, we gave ourselves a "military-style" trim, shaving the sides clean. The next morning, at the drill square, we proudly stood in formation, only to be handed three days of extra drill (ED) for our "smart initiative."

Lessons Beyond Discipline

Looking back, my time at the IMA taught me far more than drill precision or weapon handling. It taught me the value of humility, respect for hierarchy, and the bonds of camaraderie that endure long after the academy gates close.

Though my journey at the IMA was cut short, the experiences I gathered remain etched in my heart. They shaped my character and set the foundation for the corporate battles I would later fight and win.

Internal Conflict and Decision to Leave

Despite the thrill of military life, I soon found myself grappling with a growing internal conflict. Initially, my aspiration had been to join the Air Force or the Navy, driven by a fascination with aviation and the allure of naval operations. Yet, when the time came to fill out my application forms, I inadvertently chose the Army instead. This mistake loomed large in my mind, creating a nagging sense of doubt. Was I truly in the right place?

As the weeks progressed, the competitive atmosphere intensified, fueling my self-doubt. I was passionate about serving in the military, but my heart lay with the skies and the seas rather than the land. Each passing day at IMA served as a reminder of my true aspirations, amplifying my longing for a different path. The pressure to conform and the fear of disappointing those who believed in me weighed heavily on my shoulders.

After deep reflection and countless sleepless nights, I made the heart-wrenching decision to leave the academy after just two terms. This decision was not made lightly; it involved intense soul-searching and conversations with friends who had become like family. I had to confront the harsh reality that stepping away was necessary for my mental and emotional well-being.

Leaving IMA was a bittersweet farewell. I departed with a mixture of grief for what could have been and relief in knowing that I was choosing a path aligned with my authentic self. It was a difficult but necessary acknowledgment that sometimes the most courageous step is the one that leads us away from what we thought we wanted.

As I walked away from the gates of IMA, I carried with me the invaluable lessons learned and the friendships forged during my brief time there. The principles of discipline, resilience, and camaraderie became etched in my heart. I understood that my journey was not solely defined by my time at IMA but by how I would apply these lessons in the future.

In retrospect, my experiences at the Indian Military Academy were pivotal in shaping my character. The discipline instilled, the bonds formed, and the lessons learned would accompany me as I ventured into new opportunities. While my time there was short-lived, it was nonetheless transformative, providing a foundation for the challenges and triumphs that awaited me beyond the academy's gates.

02

IN THE ARENA OF AMBITION

CHAPTER 4

Army's Loss is Hong Kong Bank's Gain

A New Chapter Begins

Leaving the Indian Military Academy (IMA) was a profound moment in my life, marking the end of a long-held dream that I had nurtured since childhood. As I stepped away from the academy's gates, a whirlwind of uncertainty and anxiety enveloped me. I had invested so much time and effort into my military aspirations, and now, I was faced with the reality of forging a new path.

Growing up in a military cantonment, my entire upbringing revolved around discussions of guns, tanks, submarines, and aircraft. The armed forces were not just a career option; they were a way of life. I had always envisioned a future where I would serve my country with pride, following in the footsteps of family members who had dedicated their lives to the military. However, my experience at IMA had revealed challenges that I had not anticipated. My desire to join the Air Force or Navy remained unfulfilled primarily due to a misstep in the form-filling process. Instead of choosing the branches that truly aligned with my passion, I found myself in a cycle of expectations and decisions that felt increasingly out of my control.

Attention to detail can shape your destiny. A small oversight, like incorrectly filling out a form, can have significant consequences and close doors to opportunities you may never get back. I learnt a lesson: always take the time to review and ensure accuracy in every step of your journey, because even the smallest actions can have lasting impacts on your future.

When I made my decision to leave IMA, people whispered rumors, speculating whether I had "run away" from the academy or if I was in love with someone. The judgment stung, especially as I missed my parents, who were posted in Tezpur, nearly 2000 miles away. In those days, communication was a slow process; letters took a fortnight to reach their destination, and the immediacy of connection was lost. I longed for their support and guidance during this tumultuous time.

It was Rajiv's mother who insisted I stay with them. This provided some solace amidst the chaos. Rajiv at that time was in Warangal pursuing his Engineering degree. His parents became guiding figures, offering me encouragement to pursue what I truly wanted, irrespective of the financial pressures or societal expectations. "You shouldn't feel obligated to rush into a job," they advised. "Focus on what makes you happy." Auntie's words resonated with me, but the looming need for self-sufficiency and societal acceptance remained a burden on my shoulders.

Seeking New Opportunities

Amidst this emotional turmoil, I felt the need to take control of my life. I held a B. Com (Hons) degree with a specialization in Economics and Business Organization, but the immediate future felt uncertain. I had attempted the Indian Civil Service Exam, but I did not clear the mains. I could have chosen to wait for another year to reappear, but the pressure was mounting. I needed to establish my independence and pursue a career.

One fateful day, while going through the newspaper, a three-line advertisement caught my attention. It was vague and did not name any bank, yet it offered an opportunity that sparked my interest. I felt a rush of excitement as I read the details, realizing that this could be my chance to enter the professional world.

With a sense of urgency, I meticulously prepared my application. Drawing on the skills I had honed at IMA—leadership, discipline, and teamwork—I crafted a cover letter that reflected my passion for finance and my desire to contribute to a reputable organization. I emphasized my academic background in economics, as well as the resilience and adaptability I had developed during my time in the military environment.

I received an invitation to appear for a written exam, and as the day approached, I felt a mixture of excitement and apprehension. The exam was straightforward and basic compared to the UPSC Combined Defence Services examination, where over 800,000 candidates compete for around 400 slots. In that context, the pressure was immense, but this exam felt manageable. As I completed the test, a sense of determination washed over me; I wanted to prove my capabilities beyond the military.

To my delight, I received a letter that I had cleared the exam. The news filled me with a renewed sense of confidence. It felt like a sign that I was making the right choice, stepping away from the expectations that had begun to suffocate me.

After successfully clearing the exam, I was called in for an interview. The atmosphere was markedly different from the IMA; it was a corporate environment, buzzing with energy and professionalism. As I entered the interview room, I could sense the anticipation in the air.

Drawing on my experiences at IMA, I presented myself with confidence. I spoke about my reasons for leaving the academy, my leadership skills, my ability to work under pressure, and the discipline I had cultivated during my time in the academy. The interviewers seemed impressed, particularly with my adaptability and eagerness to learn.

I was met with one particular comment that resonated with me: "The army's loss is HSBC's gain." It struck a chord, reaffirming that my decision to leave the military was not a failure; rather, it was an opportunity to contribute my skills in a different arena.

Days later, after clearing medicals, I received the call that would change the trajectory of my life—I was offered the position at Hong Kong Bank. A wave of relief washed over me, tempered by the acknowledgment of what I was leaving behind. I realized that I had taken a significant step toward self-sufficiency and independence.

As I embarked on this new journey, I understood that my decision to leave IMA was not a misstep; rather, it was a courageous step toward redefining my aspirations. I recognized that my upbringing had instilled in me a sense of duty and service that could manifest in various forms. While my initial dream of serving in the armed forces had not materialized as I had envisioned, I discovered that there were many ways to contribute to society. The values I learned at IMA would guide me in my new role at Hong Kong Bank, where I could positively impact people's lives through financial services.

With renewed determination, I embraced the challenge ahead. The journey was just beginning, and while I had left one chapter behind, I was ready to write the next, full of promise and possibility.

Tales from My First Job: Standing Instructions and Ice Cream Breaks

The induction week at the Ambassador Hotel was nothing short of an adventure, and not necessarily the kind you write home about. For someone fresh into the banking world, I imagined this would be an intellectual baptism, learning how the gears of finance turned. What did I know? It turned out to be a week-long monologue on "What is a Bank?" and "What are Banking Products?" As I sat through it, the conclusion dawned on me: banking seemed to be an elaborate version of "organizing things and hoping they balance."

Once the induction ended, I was assigned to the Savings Department. It had a weighty department, but in practice, no one seemed particularly keen on enlightening me about what I was supposed to do. Everyone was either swamped or couldn't be bothered with the rookie in the corner. Eventually, one officer, perhaps out of pity or the fear that I'd stare at him endlessly, took it upon himself to teach me how to prepare standing instructions.

Banking back then was completely manual. No computers, no automated systems—just sheer pen-and-paper wizardry. The officer handed me a binder, gave a brief demonstration, and said, "Get working." By noon, I had transformed into a one-man standing-instructions factory. By the time my reluctant mentor was ready for lunch, I proudly announced, "Sir. Done." He raised an eyebrow, perhaps thinking I'd only managed a handful. But when I showed him the hundred-odd vouchers I'd processed, his jaw nearly hit the floor.

Unbeknownst to me, I had prepared the standing instructions for the entire year in one go. Apparently, this wasn't the standard operating procedure. He stared at me, horrified, before muttering something about "over enthusiasm" and rushing off for his lunch break, probably to regain his composure.

As the days passed, I started meeting my colleagues. That's when things got interesting—and slightly confusing. Every introduction went something like, "Hi, I'm KS Mathur." Or, "Good morning, I am MS Mathur here." Occasionally, I'd get a break with an AK Gupta, but honestly, I began to wonder if this was a Hong Kong bank or some sort of family-run enterprise. After a bit of digging, I realized many of them were indeed related, either by blood or marriage.

Being a foreign bank, we catered to a niche crowd: air hostesses, pilots, and ship captains, mostly. I vividly remember how some of the male staff would suddenly transform into their most charming selves whenever a glamorous air hostess walked in. They'd go out of their way to impress, sometimes comically so. Watching their antics became an unintentional part of my on-the-job entertainment.

My next posting was in the Remittances Department. If the Savings Department had been my trial by fire, this was my introduction to the world of peculiar banking habits. There was one businessman who made life... interesting. He had a peculiar business: buying imported cars at government auctions. Every few days, he'd sweep into the branch and demand over a hundred drafts as token money for his bids. These weren't small sums, and the process was labor-intensive.

What baffled us most was his consistency in canceling those drafts the very next day. It became such a ritual that one staff member was practically deputed full-time to manage his drafts. I often wondered if the man genuinely loved cars or just enjoyed keeping the bank on its toes. Either way, it taught me patience, or at least the art of looking patient.

Our branch was strategically located on KG Road, near Connaught Place, which was a hub of activity and charm. Lunchtimes were often spent gallivanting in CP, a ritual that gave us a much-needed break from the monotony of ledgers and vouchers. It became our little slice of paradise in the middle of a bustling workday. We'd indulge in ice cream at Nirula's, the ultimate treat after a long morning, or sip cold coffee at DePaul's, which felt like the nectar of the gods on hot Delhi afternoons.

Evenings had their own rhythm. Wenger's was a favorite haunt, where their pastries and patties never failed to lift our spirits. On days when we felt particularly extravagant, we'd head to Regal Restaurant for a proper sit-down meal. CP wasn't just a location—it was an experience. Its charm and vibrancy became an integral part of our working lives, a reminder that even in the hustle of banking, there was always time to enjoy the simpler pleasures.

Over the next few years, the landscape of our branch started to shift. New faces joined the bank. This influx of fresh talent brought new energy, and the once tightly knit (and slightly nepotistic) environment began to feel more dynamic.

The most exciting chapter of my early banking career, however, was the launch of New Delhi's first ATM. Our branch had the honor of introducing this revolutionary technology to the city, and it was nothing short of a spectacle.

The ATM was like a magical box that defied everything people knew about banking. The idea that you could withdraw money without standing in a queue, filling out a withdrawal slip, or dealing with a teller was mind-boggling. News of the 'cash-dispensing machine' spread like wildfire, and people came in droves, not just to use it but to witness it in action. Some stood in line simply to press a few buttons and watch the machine spit out crisp currency notes. For them, it was an awe-inspiring technological marvel; for us, it was both a matter of pride and a bit of a headache.

Initially, there was a lot of confusion. People would insert their cards the wrong way or try to use the machine without entering a PIN. Some thought it was a clever trick and spent ages trying to figure out 'where the teller was hiding.' Others were convinced the ATM would run out of cash if it worked for too long, so they'd withdraw the smallest possible amount, just to be safe. Despite the chaos, the enthusiasm was infectious.

The ATM became a symbol of progress, and our branch became a point of curiosity and envy among the other banks. It felt incredible to be part of something that was not just changing the way people banked but also redefining the very concept of convenience. The launch of the ATM wasn't just a milestone for the bank, it was a moment of pride for all of us who worked there.

Then came my stint with the tellers. This was an eye-opener, to say the least. Handling cash meant dealing with every sort of personality under the sun—some polite, others downright impossible. Once, a customer tried to "correct" my cash counting, insisting I was a rupee off. I knew I wasn't. But after a brief argument and a coin toss (figuratively, not literally), I counted again, right in front of him. It was perfect, of course. He smiled sheepishly, muttered something about "bad eyesight," and left.

By the time I moved to Guarantee Issuance, I had developed a thick skin and a knack for navigating quirks, both human and procedural. Guarantees were serious business, often involving large sums and high stakes. But even here, moments of humor weren't rare. One client, after a lengthy discussion, handed over a set of documents with a flourish, saying, "It's all here, triple-checked!" Only for me to find out he had submitted the wrong forms entirely. His embarrassed laugh still rings in my ears.

Somewhere along the way, having completed 3-year eligibility criteria in the bank, I decided to sit for the promotion exam. It wasn't an easy process—there was preparation to be done, and plenty of approvals to wade through. The exam itself was a mix of practical banking knowledge and abstract reasoning, designed to test not just what we knew, but how we thought. I emerged reasonably confident, but promotions in a bank weren't just about passing exams. Vacancies dictated everything.

When the results came, I was shortlisted. "Subject to vacancy," the note said. It was a bittersweet moment. I had made the cut, but there was no guarantee when—or if—a promotion would come.

Between the new faces, the iconic CP breaks, and the unprecedented buzz of the ATM, my early years in banking were far from ordinary. Each day brought something new—a laugh, a lesson, or a little piece of history in the making. Looking back, those days were formative, not just in my career but in shaping how I saw the world. Banking wasn't just about handling money; it was about embracing change, adapting to surprises, and finding joy in the everyday. And if you had Nirula's ice cream or DePaul's cold coffee to go with it, well, that was just the cherry on top.

A New Beginning at Chandni Chowk Branch

On April 1, 1988, at 9 AM, I received the exhilarating news: I had been promoted and was to report immediately to our Chandni Chowk branch. The excitement of the promotion was quickly tempered by anxiety; I had no idea where the branch was located. After asking a few colleagues, I learned that taking a cycle rickshaw would be the best way to navigate through the bustling commercial area, which would soon be choked with traffic. With my belongings and lunch packed, I set off.

Finding the branch was no easy task. After asking several people for directions, I received vague assurances that it was nearby. Without the convenience of mobile phones, my frustration grew. Just when I thought I might never find it, I approached a Panipuri (crispy fried stuffed spicy water ball) vendor. Unlike the others, he didn't just nod in affirmation. Instead, he pointed skyward. Curious, I looked up and spotted a signboard perched atop a shop —Bata Store!

It turned out the branch was located on the first and second floors.

As I tried to climb the narrow staircase, I was met with an overwhelming sight: a narrow corridor packed with over a hundred people waiting in line. It was just before 10 AM, just moments before the bank's gates were to open. I was told to stand in the queue. I tried explaining them that I work for the bank, but was given a state. Resigned yet amused, I came out, stood in the queue, and after half an hour or so, I finally reported to the branch manager, Mr. J N Saxena. A seasoned banker, he had heard of my reputation and was keen to see how I would tackle this immediate challenge.

"Why don't you solve this issue?" he suggested, a hint of a challenge in his voice. It was a familiar refrain: never throw a problem at an army man; he will find a solution. I agreed and asked for a week to study the situation and devise a plan.

As I observed the branch's operations, I quickly realized that Chandni Chowk was a commercial hub. Our clientele consisted primarily of wholesalers and distributors, ranging from textiles to grains to bullion to electrical to electronics. Being the only foreign bank in the area, having an account with us was prestigious.

Each morning, just before businesses opened, accountants would flood in to deposit cheques and drafts collected during the previous day. This rush occurred because the clearing of these instruments was accepted until noon, which put pressure on everyone to deposit as early as possible. However, with only two tellers handling the influx, the process was slow and inefficient.

Recognizing the bottleneck, I reached out to our head office, proposing that we not print receipts for every customer copy. Instead, I suggested we allow any bank officer to sign and stamp a single customer acknowledgment copy.

To my delight, the dispensation was approved.

The next day, armed with my pen and the bank's official stamp, I stationed myself at the foot of the stairs leading to the branch. As the accountants and clients arrived, I checked their deposit slips, and signed and stamped acknowledgments,

Miraculously, by 10:30 AM, the long queues had vanished. Customers began to call the manager, complaining about my new process, but JNS reassured them that all was well.

As the branch began to take on a new atmosphere—where there had once been chaos, there was now calm—the relief was palpable. However, the issue didn't end there. While I had alleviated the immediate concern of customer wait times, our tellers faced a new challenge. We received around 1,000 deposit slips daily, totaling an average of 3,000 cheques and drafts. The tellers, overwhelmed by the volume, protested to their union.

Once again, I tapped into my military experience to find a solution. Rather than handing the deposit slips directly to the tellers, I reversed the process. I instructed two of my staff, both seasoned clerks who were nearing retirement, to verify details of each deposit slip against its accompanying cheques and drafts. They were to cross check tally and organize these slips into batches of 50 and handed the corresponding instruments to the encoding team while returning the slips to the tellers for posting.

This shift transformed the entire process. The tellers, who had previously felt overwhelmed, found themselves with idle time and began requesting more slips to process. From a situation fraught with customer inconvenience and delays in submitting clearances to the Reserve Bank of India, we successfully completed the entire process by 2.30 PM. In addition, we extended the time to deposit such instruments till banking hours i.e. 2 PM,

By the time my first month was up, the branch was running like a well-oiled machine. The old guard had transformed into a motivated team, and I had learned that sometimes, a little patience, a lot of empathy, and a sense of humor could turn even the most challenging situations into successes. With this newfound efficiency, I received numerous requests from tellers wanting to join my department.

My ability to utilize resources optimally and motivate my team had made a significant impact. I was reminded of the invaluable lessons I had learned in the army: effective leadership involves understanding the strengths of your team and utilizing them to achieve common goals.

My experiences at the Chandni Chowk branch not only strengthened my banking skills but also reinforced the importance of community and collaboration. I had transitioned from being an army officer to a banker, and with that came new challenges and opportunities for growth. The relationships I built during this period would prove essential, laying the foundation for my future endeavors in the banking world. Embracing the unique atmosphere of Chandni Chowk, I was not just a banker; I was part of a community, learning and evolving alongside my clients and colleagues.

Looking back, those early days at the Chandni Chowk branch taught me more than any training program ever could. And every time I think about that hidden first-floor bank and the queue of a hundred merchants, I can't help but smile.

Marriage Proposal and Mishaps

It was a night like any other when I had the misfortune of meeting with an accident on my way home. Nothing too catastrophic—just a few bruises on my face, hands, and a bandaged head, giving me the appearance of a warrior who had survived an epic battle. It wasn't the most flattering look, but it did the job of keeping the nosy neighbors at bay. I decided to take a few days off from work to recuperate, figuring a little time to rest might do wonders for both my body and my dignity.

However, my injury did little to slow the events that were about to unfold in my life. One morning, we had visitors. They were introduced as the brother and mother of a prospective bride. At first, I wasn't sure what to make of the situation—was this a set-up? A match made by my parents, or was I unknowingly walking into some elaborate game of familial matchmaking? I didn't have long to ponder, because the visitors, having seen my bandaged face and head, seemed surprisingly unfazed. The mother and brother were carrying a passport-sized photograph of the girl—an innocent picture of a young woman, though I couldn't see how her expression would align with my bruised visage. They assured us that the match looked good, and before I could formulate any thoughts, they invited us to visit their house to meet the girl.

A few weeks later, we went to their home. It was an awkward situation. I had a feeling that things were moving too fast, but then again, maybe it was just my bruises that made me feel uncomfortable. When we arrived, the girl's bhabi (sister-in-law) asked me to step into another room. I thought maybe she wanted to talk to me privately, or perhaps the girl wanted to have a conversation. But no. Instead, they asked us to stand side by side. "Anju believes you are shorter than her," she said, scrutinizing the difference in our heights. It turned out that I was 4 inches taller, which evidently brought relief to the family. In their minds, this minor issue had been a critical test of compatibility.

Without so much as a question, they proceeded to confirm their approval. My parents, eager and resolute, declared that the match was a green light. "Yes," they said, without even bothering to wait for my opinion. It all happened so quickly, almost too quickly for my liking. The decision had been made, but I hadn't even spoken to the girl yet. How could they approve something without knowing whether we were even compatible beyond our heights?

The very next day, as I sat at my office desk, still processing the events from the previous evening, I couldn't shake the nagging feeling of uncertainty. How could they decide something as important as marriage without a proper conversation between us? It wasn't right. So, I decided to take matters into my own hands. I left the bank early and decided to visit the school where the girl was working. I thought I'd get a glimpse of her, maybe even say a few words before anything more was set in stone.

I stood outside her school long before the bell rang. There I was, awkwardly waiting like some sort of adolescent trying to impress a crush, but instead of a heartwarming moment, I was left looking like a fool. Finally, the school bell rang, and she appeared, completely unaware of my nervous anticipation. She glanced at me, and without so much as a word, hopped onto the first school bus and disappeared into the distance. I stood there, feeling like a monkey that had just made a fool of himself. My grand plan had failed miserably.

The next day, I got a call from her brother. He had caught wind of my impromptu visit and seemed to understand my dilemma. I explained myself, and to my relief, he wasn't offended. Instead, he kindly suggested that I meet the girl over coffee. "No pressure," he said. "Just a conversation." That was how we ended up going on our first date.

Over the next few months, we met frequently, and what started as a tentative coffee date soon turned into something more genuine. We dated every day, and within four months, we were married. It was a whirlwind romance, or perhaps, a whirlwind decision, depending on how you looked at it. All I knew was that there had to be something special about her for me to take such a bold step, especially after such an awkward beginning

Throughout this period, I had the unwavering support of my manager, who understood the gravity of the situation. He encouraged me to leave early for our dates, so long as I finished my work. "Savor this time," he said with a knowing smile. "Once you're married, things will be different." He was right, of course. Life did change after marriage, but that's a story for another day.

As I look back on the entire experience, one thing that still boggles my mind is how my future in-laws could have agreed to the marriage so quickly, without ever having a proper conversation with me. My father-in-law, ever the diplomat, later shared something that added another layer of comedy to the situation.

It turns out, before meeting us at home, my father-in-law had discreetly visited my branch at Chandni Chowk. He wanted to inquire about me without tipping anyone off. I'm still trying to figure out who the staff member was who spoke with him, but according to my father-in-law, the conversation went something like this: "Sir, if I had a sister, I would have married her to him." Brand equity, they called it. Apparently, my reputation at work was enough to convince him that I was a good match, despite the fact that my face looked like a battle wound at the time.

This anecdote still makes me chuckle. In hindsight, the whole affair was a perfect storm of miscommunication, awkwardness, and improbable trust. My in-laws, in their wisdom, saw something in me that I had yet to discover in myself. And while the journey to marriage was unconventional, it led me to a place I could never have predicted.

Reflecting on all this, I can't help but wonder: How often do we judge situations or people based on assumptions, reputation, or external appearances? How many decisions do we make without truly understanding what's behind the surface? Perhaps there's a lesson in the way my marriage began. Maybe it's about trusting in the process, even when the path isn't entirely clear.

After all, if a family can make a life-altering decision based on a few words from a staff member, surely, we can learn to trust our instincts, and sometimes, take a leap of faith ourselves.

Travel Trails – The Road Runner

Chandni Chowk greeted first-timers with the chaotic symphony of honking horns, shouting vendors, and the constant hustle of crowded streets. Each day, the vibrant energy of the area pulsed around me—a unique blend of history and modernity interlaced with daily struggles. I had recently been transferred to an office branch located amidst this urban chaos, and commuting to work transformed into a daily challenge of its own.

Living across town meant that I had no direct connectivity to the office, forcing me into the labyrinth of public transportation. My attempts at catching buses often proved futile; delays became the unwelcome norm, and I found myself spending more time waiting than traveling. Frustrated with my long hours in overcrowded buses, I made a decision that would change my commuting experience: I would begin traversing the streets of Chandni Chowk on a two-wheeler.

Riding through the narrow lanes and bustling streets during evening rush hour felt akin to stepping into a chaotic arena. The scene was a pulsing mess of cars, mini trucks, auto-rickshaws, cycle rickshaws, bullock carts, hand carts, and pedestrians, all vying for the same slivers of space on the road. It was a test—one where survival required agility, quick thinking, and perhaps a dash of insanity.

Each ride was a rollercoaster of emotions; I often had to duck, swerve, brake, and accelerate just to navigate the maze of vehicles that seemed to multiply with every passing minute. Blasting horns amalgamated with shouts from street vendors and the laughter of children, creating a cacophony that made every journey feel like a battleground. The frenetic energy of Chandni Chowk was overwhelming and exhilarating all at once.

Despite the initial terror of riding through such chaos, I gradually adapted and began to master the art of navigating the streets. It required resilience, determination, and finely tuned reflexes. I learned to predict the behavior of other drivers and developed a keen sense of timing to maneuver through narrow alleys and congested roads knowing very well that bullock carts had no brakes. Each day's journey became a ritual of proving my perseverance amidst a sea of hurdles, with my spirits lifting as I increasingly felt like a part of this vibrant society.

As challenging as my daily commute was, the sense of accomplishment and satisfaction that washed over me as I reached my destination safely became addictive. Every successful arrival felt like a personal victory—a small yet significant triumph against the odds stacked against me. Commuting through the congested commercial area of Chandni Chowk had morphed into a thrilling adventure—an essential part of my day.

However, it wasn't just my personal escapades that added to the unique tapestry of life in Chandni Chowk. One day, my wife decided to join me on a shopping trip to this bustling hub. Her excitement was palpable; she had heard tales of the rich variety of goods available at unbelievably low prices, and she wanted to experience it firsthand. As we move through the crowded lanes, she marveled at the colorful displays of textiles, jewelry, and street food that filled every nook and cranny. The alluring smells of spices and sweets drew her in like a moth to a flame, and soon we were sampling an array of delightful delicacies, each boasting its own distinctive taste and flavor.

But the return journey was where the thrill of the day turned from exhilarating to downright terrifying. As I mounted my two-wheeler, my wife clutched my waist tightly, her excitement slowly giving way to anxiety. The streets that had once appeared vibrant were now buzzing with an overwhelming intensity. As I navigated through the congestion, every swerve and brake felt like a plunge on a roller coaster—sharp and unpredictable. With every honk and near-miss, I felt her grip tighten. "This is worse than any amusement park ride!" she exclaimed through a nervous giggle, trying to mask her fear. My own heart raced as I zigzagged through the disarray, each maneuver feeling like a high-wire act without a safety net. Her laughter soon turned into squeals as we hit a potholed area that jolted us in every direction.

Finally, we arrived home, and she clambered off my bike with the grace of a catapulted kangaroo. Breathless and wide-eyed, she turned to me and exclaimed, "Never. Ever. Again!" All of her earlier joy drained away, replaced by a palpable resolve to never tackle the chaos of Chandni Chowk's streets again. Her adventurous spirit, once eager to taste the charm of the busy market, had encountered its limits.

In the days that followed, I would hint at her joining me for a quick ride, only to see her shake her head vigorously, a hint of a smile still lingering as she recalled our tumultuous trip. I would chuckle; she was too intertwined with the cozy comfort of home, opting instead for the tranquility of online shopping.

Chandni Chowk, despite its challenges, had become a statement of resilience in my life—a nerve-wracking but thrilling journey reminiscent of a vibrant carnival. What started as a daily commute morphed into a tale woven with the fabric of urban life, filled with trials, victories, and memorable adventures. In its chaotic embrace, I found not just the daily grind, but a story worth savoring.

A New Challenge: The Call to Mumbai

Hong Kong Bank was now rebranded as HSBC.

With the success I achieved at the Chandni Chowk branch, my reputation as a problem-solver and leader began to grow. I was recognized not just for my military background but for my ability to apply those lessons in a corporate setting. As the dust settled on my initial months at HSBC, I was presented with an exciting opportunity to take on a new challenge that would further expand my horizons.

In Dec 1992, after my success at Chandni Chowk, I received a call from the Retail Banking Manager's office of HSBC, inviting me to Mumbai for a special assignment focused on a technology upgrade project. The move was significant; it represented not just a change in location but a shift in responsibility. I was both anxious and excited. Moving from branch operations to a pivotal role in technology integration was a leap, and I would be stepping into a world filled with strategic planning and cross-departmental collaboration.

As I transitioned into this new role, I quickly realized that I had much to learn. The banking world was evolving rapidly, and the full automation of banking software and systems was at the forefront of this transformation. I dove headfirst into understanding various systems and processes, collaborating closely with IT professionals and other departments. My background in the military taught me the value of adaptability and quick learning—skills that would serve me well in this new environment.

The team I joined was dynamic and driven, consisting of talented individuals from diverse backgrounds. It was inspiring to be part of a group where everyone was committed to innovation and improvement. Together, we explored how to streamline processes, reduce manual errors, and enhance customer service through state-of-the-art technology.

A Major Project: Implementing a New Banking System

One of the most significant projects I led was the implementation of this new banking software system designed to unify our operations across various branches. This project required meticulous planning, coordination, and training. This meant a complete overhaul: everything changed, from account numbers to customer groupings and unique customer IDs. The complexity of the project required seamless collaboration with stakeholders, staff, and customers alike.

Despite the magnitude of the project, we had to ensure that the bank never ceased operations. It was akin to performing a heart transplant—everything had to continue beating smoothly while we made these critical changes. We were determined to maintain uninterrupted service for our customers. I took it upon myself to communicate the vision and benefits of this new system to every level of staff, from executives to front-line tellers.

The introduction of the new banking system in 1994 significantly transformed our operations. Transaction times decreased, errors were minimized, and customer satisfaction improved. Clients praised the enhanced online banking services, which made their lives easier. It was gratifying to see our hard work come to fruition, knowing that we were making a real difference in our customers' experiences.

As I reflect on this journey, I realize how much I had grown, not just as a banker but as a leader. The ability to adapt, inspire, and unite a team toward a common goal became my greatest asset. I felt a deep sense of fulfillment in knowing that I was contributing to a more efficient, customer-focused banking experience.

Building Relationships

Throughout my time in Mumbai, I forged strong relationships with colleagues from different locations. I valued these connections, as they provided insights into the needs and expectations of our customers. I also learned that effective leadership isn't just about implementing changes; it's about fostering a culture of collaboration and open communication. In this chapter of my career, I wasn't just an army man turned banker; I was a change agent, committed to driving innovation and excellence in an industry that was constantly evolving. My experiences in Mumbai set the stage for the next phase of my career, where I would continue to learn, lead, and make a lasting impact in the world of banking.

Trade Services: Lessons of Perfectionism

In April 1994, I was promoted and relocated back to the corporate office in New Delhi. The move signaled a new chapter in my banking career, bringing with it fresh responsibilities and opportunities for growth. I was now in the Trade Services department, a critical role in the bank's corporate division, little did I know that this period would not only sharpen my technical skills but also test my resilience and challenge the very core of my professional journey.

Working with Tarun: Mentorship and Leadership

One of the most significant experiences in this phase was working with Tarun, who was heading the Imports business. He had a reputation for his sharp strategic mind and leadership acumen. Tarun had an exceptional ability to cut through complexity and deliver results without compromising on ethics or professionalism. Under his mentorship, I began to understand the importance of strategic thinking and the need for a balance between operational efficiency and leadership.

He didn't believe in micro-management. Instead, he trusted his team to deliver and gave them the freedom to explore new ideas. This trust allowed me to take on larger responsibilities within the Imports department. I learned from him how to navigate the balance between team empowerment and accountability. He expected me to not only remember each and every section of Uniform Codes and Practice for International trade, by heart, but more importantly to apply it. We sharpened UCP sections by having quiz sessions after lunch break. I learnt how crucial and critical it was for international trade finance. It wasn't just about bills of payment and Letter of credits; it was about leading a cohesive team that took ownership of their work on behalf of the bank and customer's trust.

Tarun's leadership also inspired me to push my limits. His encouragement and the respect he showed his team made me want to not only meet but exceed expectations. He knew how to bring out the best in people, and this was a trait I knew I had to adopt in my own leadership journey.

Facing the Audit: A Baptism of Fire

Not long after joining the Trade Services department, I had my first major test—a comprehensive audit of the department's operations. The audit was thorough and detailed, scrutinizing every aspect of our processes, compliance, and internal controls. The audit team was notorious for being stringent, and there was no room for error. It was, in every sense, a baptism of fire.

While I had always been a stickler for compliance, this experience forced me to dig deeper. It wasn't just about ticking boxes; it was about ensuring that every process and transaction was airtight. The previous auditors in the last audit had highlighted several areas where the department needed improvement. I had worked closely with my team to address the audit findings. We streamlined processes, strengthened internal controls, and ensured that every compliance requirement was met.

The audit went on smoothly with no adverse comments. The work was intense, but it paid off. Our department had not only met the regulatory and internal control requirements but had set a new benchmark for efficiency and compliance.

The experience taught me two invaluable lessons. First, the importance of attention to detail in every aspect of operations, especially in a field as sensitive as trade services. Second, the importance of staying calm under pressure.

The Fight Against Perception Bias

However, the most significant challenge I faced during this period wasn't operational—it was personal. Despite my strong performance and meeting eligibility criteria, I wasn't initially nominated for the bank's prestigious RM Assessment Centre, a program designed to identify and groom future leaders within the organization. The Assessment Centre was a rigorous process that evaluated candidates on various aspects of leadership, decision-making, and problem-solving.

I soon learned that a mix of bias and office politics had influenced the decision to leave me out of the nominations. It was disappointing, to say the least. I had worked hard, delivered results, and earned the respect of my peers and superiors. But here I was, being passed over for an opportunity I knew I deserved.

Instead of letting frustration get the better of me, I chose to fight the bias. I requested a meeting with Tarun, where I calmly but firmly made my case. I pointed to my track record, my contributions to the bank, and the results I had delivered. Tarun supported and took up my case, and after multiple discussions, my nomination was finally accepted.

The Assessment Centre itself was a formidable challenge. For two days, we were assessed on various aspects of management and leadership under of watchful eyes of experienced assessors. I reminisced about my SSB interview days while waiting for the Board to announce results.

A secretary from HR walked into the meeting room where I was waiting. She told me that Sumit Sharma from HR wants me to see him immediately. Now, if you've ever received a call from HR, you know that feeling—your stomach does a little flip, and you start running through a mental checklist. "What have I done wrong?"

Sumit with a grim look, asked me. "You could have done better, Anil." I was shocked. Suddenly, he burst out laughing. "Congratulations! You've been selected for the Executive Trainee Development Program!"

Out of 12 candidates, I was the only one to clear the process. It was a vindication of my abilities and a powerful reminder that persistence pays off. I had fought for the opportunity to prove myself, and when the time came, I delivered.

The journey to the Assessment Centre and the ultimate success wasn't just a professional milestone; it was a deeply personal victory. It reaffirmed my belief in my own capabilities and reinforced the importance of resilience and perseverance in the face of adversity. Being the only one to clear the Assessment Centre out of 16 candidates wasn't just a professional triumph—it was a validation of the values that had shaped me throughout my career: integrity, hard work, and never giving up.

My heart did a little jig. I was in! The dance was quickly interrupted when he mentioned, almost as an afterthought, that I needed to be in the UK in two weeks. Bricketwood, St. Albans, to be exact.

The excitement of clearing the assessment center was just beginning to sink in. It felt like I'd finally climbed the first step of a steep ladder. Oh, and one more thing. I'd need to submit my passport for the visa process.

A tiny detail, right? Except, I didn't have a passport. I'm not talking about an expired one or a lost one—no, I had never owned one. The most 'international' trip I had ever taken was Nepal.

To make matters worse, in those days, getting a passport wasn't the streamlined, online-appointment process it is now. It took about three to four months, and that's if all your documents were in order, and subject to police clearance I was facing a two-week deadline with a process that usually took a quarter of a year.

Things weren't looking good. So, I did what any self-respecting Indian would do in a crisis—I called my aunt. Now, my aunt was not just any aunt; she worked in the Ministry, which, to me, sounded incredibly important, though I wasn't entirely sure what they did.

After hearing my predicament, my aunt decided to help. She whisked me away to meet her boss, a joint secretary. I didn't know much about joint secretaries, but judging by the number of phones on his desk, I figured he was important. The joint secretary, a man who clearly valued efficiency, listened to my aunt's explanation of my situation and responded with a thoughtful "Hmmm." He then proceeded to make a series of phone calls with a level of calm that seemed almost magical. At the end of his brief conversation, he simply said, "Let's go." Just like that.

No explanation. No reassurance. Just a very confident, "Let's go."

I assumed he had a plan, but I didn't want to ask too many questions. When someone in a position of power says "let's go," you don't argue—you just go. Now, since his official car wasn't available, I did the next best thing: I offered him a ride on my scooter.

Yes, that's right.

A joint secretary in the Indian government hopped onto the back of my trusty Bajaj scooter like it was the most normal thing in the world. If you've ever ridden through the chaotic streets of Chandni Chowk on a two-wheeler, you'll know it's not for the faint-hearted. But here I was, weaving through central vista roads, with a senior government official clinging to the back seat. It was a sight to behold: me, with my "made-in-India" scooter, and him, in a crisply ironed suit, zooming past cars and autorickshaws, and the occasional bus. If you've never dodged a jaywalker while transporting a high-ranking official, I highly recommend it. It builds character. We arrived at another majestic central government building, the heart of Indian bureaucracy, and entered an office that felt more like a small palace.

We were ushered into a room that belonged to another high-ranking officer, a course mate of the joint secretary.

After a brief introduction, and what seemed to be another cryptic series of "Hmmm" sounds, a call was made. Next thing I knew, I was being told to head over to the passport office to meet a certain Mr. X.

Mr. X?

I dropped the joint secretary back at his office (the ride back was significantly more relaxed), and then I raced to the passport office, at Bhikaji Cama Place, my nerves now getting the better of me. Upon arrival, I nervously mentioned Mr. X's name to the receptionist, half expecting to be laughed out of the building. But, to my surprise, I was immediately escorted to an imposing office. There, I met the Mr. X—a man who looked enigmatic. Mr. X glanced at my application, nodded, and said, "Submit at counter no 10. Come back at 5." That's it.

No further explanation. I submitted the application, it was scrutinized by the official, I was directed to deposit the fees. I was left in a daze. But like clockwork, I returned at 5, not knowing what to expect.

To my astonishment, I was handed a brand-new, shiny passport. I stood there, blinking, as if it might disappear if I looked away for too long. It was still warm, like it had just been printed, which it probably had. I couldn't believe it.

In a matter of hours, I had done what usually takes months. Was it luck? Was it destiny? Or was it the result of riding around Delhi on a scooter with a government official? I'd like to think it was a little bit of all three.

As I clutched my passport, ready to embark on this new chapter of life, I couldn't help but reflect on the whirlwind of events that led to this moment. Who knew that getting a passport could involve so much drama, suspense, and a scooter ride through New Delhi diplomatic area. It was one of those days where the universe seemed to align in my favor. Either that or I was the lucky beneficiary of some serious bureaucratic magic. Either way, I was ready for the next adventure—Bricketwood, here I come!

As I boarded the aircraft to London, I reflected on my journey. Returning to New Delhi and leading the Trade Services department was one of the most defining periods of my career. From working under Tarun Balram's leadership to handling the audit and fighting bias to secure my place at the Assessment Centre, each episodexperience contributed to my growth, both as a professional and as a leader.

This chapter in my career set the tone for the next phase of my professional journey, where I would not only lead but also mentor and develop the next generation of leaders. The lessons I learned in this period, —about persistence, fairness, and leadership, —would continue to shape my decisions and actions for years to come.

The Art of Immigration: A Lesson in Patience and Persistence

With a freshly stamped UK Visa in my passport in hand, and a mix of excitement and anxiety bubbling within, I kissed my wife goodbye on the 15th of August and boarded a flight bound for Heathrow Airport. A journey that, for most, might be routine, for me, was the beginning of a new chapter – one that would eventually define my career.

Little did I know, however, that the adventure would begin far before I set foot on the picturesque campus of my management program. The flight itself was pleasant enough, if you don't count the baby crying two rows behind me, the elderly man who snored like a malfunctioning chainsaw, and the in-flight meal, which seemed to be a curious attempt at "food." But hey, an eight-hour flight isn't supposed to be a five-star experience, right?

I arrived at Heathrow at precisely 7 a.m., bleary-eyed but filled with the optimism that only comes when you think your international journey is about to proceed like clockwork.

How wrong I was.

Heathrow Airport, for those of you who have never had the pleasure, is a beast unto itself. A massive, sprawling city disguised as an airport where the uninitiated are frequently eaten alive by long queues, strange accents, and perplexing signs.

But there I was, armed with nothing but my suitcase, a hopeful attitude, and absolutely no means of contacting anyone. It was the early 1996, and mobile phones were not the ubiquitous appendages they are today. If I had needed to send an urgent message, I would have had better luck training a carrier pigeon. The airport was already buzzing with activity despite the early hour. I made my way through the terminal, head held high, searching for the designated pickup area where, according to the email I had read far too many times, a driver would be waiting for me. In hindsight, I probably should have memorized the poor man's face, or at least his name. But no, I had complete faith in my ability to simply... find him.

My confidence in this plan would soon be tested. But before I could even reach the mystical pickup area, I had to go through immigration. Now, if there's one thing I've learned from my travels, it's that immigration officials are rarely in a rush. These are individuals who hold your fate in their hands, and they know it. So, naturally, there were two queues: one moving at a reasonable pace, and the other... well, the other moved with the velocity of a glacier trying to cross a desert.

Guess which line I was in.

As I stood there, shifting my weight from one foot to the other, I mentally prepared myself for what would surely be a standard interaction. I imagined myself breezing through immigration, nodding politely at the official, and exiting triumphantly to find my driver with time to spare. Unfortunately, the universe had other plans.

When it was finally my turn, I approached the immigration counter with what I hoped was an expression of calm, collected authority. The official, however, was not impressed by my aura of confidence. He took my passport, flipped through it as though he were searching for hidden secrets, and then, without a word, motioned for me to wait in a separate area.

Now, let me paint a picture of this waiting area. It wasn't exactly the warm, welcoming corner I had envisioned. There were few chairs. One was occupied by a man from Romania (as per the passport he was holding), who was apparently having an intense conversation with his phone. Loudly. If you've never had the experience of listening to a heated conversation in a language you don't understand while simultaneously wondering if you're about to be deported, I assure you, it's a memorable one.

The minutes stretched into what felt like hours. Officials came and went, each throwing me a glance that seemed to say, "Ah, another one." My mind began racing. Had I done something wrong?

Finally, after what seemed like an eternity (but was probably closer to 45 minutes), a senior official summoned me. He explained, in a tone that suggested he had seen this all before, that there was "a slight issue" with my passport. My heart sank. A slight issue? What did that even mean? Was I about to be sent back home without so much as a cup of English tea?

With the enthusiasm of a man whose life depended on it, I explained that my passport had been issued just the week before, specifically for my enrollment in the prestigious HSBC management program. Surely that counted for something? I'm not sure if it was my impassioned speech or their need to free up a chair for the next victim, but eventually, after much back-and-forth, they verified my passport, made some calls, and allowed me to proceed.

Victory, at last!

Except... by now, two hours had passed, and I had missed my pickup. At this point, I was equal parts relieved and frazzled. I withdrew some cash from an ATM (the most comforting sound in the world at that moment) and managed to call the driver. To my great relief, he informed me that he was about to enter the campus but was on his way back to collect me. Finally, something was going right.

When I arrived at the campus, any lingering frustration melted away. The place was beautiful, an oasis of academic splendor. My batchmates, hailing from 14 different countries, greeted me with warmth and enthusiasm. The chaotic start to my journey was quickly forgotten as I settled into this new environment, ready to embrace the adventure ahead.

Looking back, that immigration fiasco taught me more than any classroom could. It was a lesson in patience, persistence, and the importance of carrying snacks (because you never know how long you'll be stuck in an airport). And so, with a heart full of optimism and just a little bit of jet lag, I stepped into the next chapter of my story, ready to tackle whatever challenges came my way – just as long as they didn't involve any more immigration lines.

London Life

Life at Bricketwood was unlike anything I had ever experienced before, and believe me, I've had my share of adventures. The

HSBC Training College wasn't just a facility where people sharpened their banking skills—it was a mini cosmos of cultures, personalities, and unexpected moments that made each day feel like a quirky new episode of a global sitcom. Imagine a sprawling 184-acre campus nestled in the English countryside, complete with a state-of-the-art sports complex, scenic walking trails, and a lake so serene it could calm a room full of caffeine-fueled traders.

The campus was a bustling hub, with HSBC employees from all corners of the globe arriving wide-eyed and eager to learn. It was a hive of activity, a place where strategy and spreadsheets met laughter, learning, and, at times, a lot of confusion over British accents. I was there to develop my banking and leadership knowledge, but what I didn't expect was how this place would pull me into a whirlwind of camaraderie, cultural exchanges, and peculiar bonding rituals (more on that later).

Of course, a major highlight was the college's restaurant, aptly named The Melting Pot. The place was a culinary and conversational battleground where delegates from more than 40 countries gathered for meals. It wasn't just about food—it was about the stories, ideas, and in some cases, debates, shared over dinner. I sat next to people who had stories about growing up in Singapore, banking in Mexico, infrastructure marvels of China, and even surviving extreme winters in Canada.

Once, during dessert, we had a heated argument over whether real Italian pizza should be crispy or soft, which ended when an Italian colleague stood up dramatically and stormed out, appalled at our lack of cultural sophistication. In my cohort, we had 15 delegates from 10 different countries, and while we might have initially struggled to understand each other's accents, by the second week we were practically finishing each other's sentences, or at least laughing at each other's misunderstandings.

No wonder Hindi became most popular language. During one particularly memorable dinner, a Saudi colleague misunderstood the phrase "barking up the wrong tree" as "barking like a tree"—which, let's face it, doesn't even make sense—but it left us all in stitches for days. Our dining room banter felt less like a formal training program and more like the setup for a global comedy show.

Our accommodation was in the Lakeside Block, which lived up to its name by being positioned next to a calm, glassy lake. It was picturesque, and the view could easily trick you into thinking you were at a wellness retreat rather than a grueling training program. Some evenings, I'd sit by the lake, pretending to review my notes but actually contemplating the deeper mysteries of life, like why the British insist on putting butter on their sandwiches or whether I could survive on nothing but fish and chips for a week (spoiler: I couldn't).

But let's talk about the serious stuff: the outbound group-building exercises. These were designed to forge unity and trust, though at times, it felt like we were contestants on a global version of Survivor. In one particularly challenging exercise, we were split into two groups and asked to navigate a series of obstacles in the woods.

Our group, nicknamed the "Lost Causes" (an endearing moniker, I assure you), was tasked with figuring out how to make a raft with empty petrol cans and few planks. Everyone thought they are like Robinson Crusoe. It became less about physical strength and more about teamwork and understanding accents, although there was a terrifying moment when one overly enthusiastic team member decided to hoist himself on the raft, shouting, "I believe in you guys!" Let's just say his faith in us was misplaced. The raft turned turtle.

The classroom sessions were equally intense, but instead of jungle gyms, we were tackling complex subjects: banking, treasury, international trade, finance, management, and the ever-dreaded financial regulations. These weren't your typical lectures. Our instructors were masters of their craft, adept at making even the dullest topics (like accounting) seem like something out of a suspense thriller.

I was especially impressed by my Chinese classmates, who initially struggled with English but, by week 12, were debating financial policies in flawless English. The Singaporeans, on the other hand, were meticulous. They took notes as if their lives depended on capturing every single word. I'm pretty sure some of them could have recited entire lessons verbatim by the end. Of course, after these intense days, we all needed to unwind.

Enter the pub—a quintessentially British establishment that became our go-to for post-class debriefs. Over pints of beer (and occasionally something stronger), we shared stories, vented about the day's challenges, and laughed until our sides hurt. If you want to understand the spirit of global bonding, imagine an Australian, a Sri Lankan, and an Indian passionately discussing cricket rules over a plate of fish and chips. The British colleagues watched in amusement as we gestured wildly, using wrists and hands to demonstrate different strokes and spins.

Weekends were a special treat. We would head out to explore nearby cities, soaking up the local culture and history. I remember one Saturday when we all went to London. A bunch of bankers, armed with maps and an appalling lack of direction, trying to navigate the Tube—it was a sight to behold. We spent the day in awe of landmarks like the Tower of London and Buckingham Palace, but the real highlight was our attempt to blend in with locals by attempting the British art of queuing. Let's just say the experience ended with an embarrassing incident involving a confused queue for the London Eye, a heated debate, and a lot of apologies to confused tourists.

As the program drew to a close, we gathered for the final dinner—this time, with the Group CEO in attendance. It was a formal affair, but the mood was bittersweet. Postings were announced, and the room buzzed with excitement and nervous anticipation. When my name was called, I felt a rush of adrenaline. Mumbai!

A new adventure awaited, and while I was thrilled, I couldn't shake the sadness of leaving this oddball group of brilliant, quirky individuals behind. We had bonded over shared challenges, strange British idioms, and a mutual love-hate relationship with English weather. Now, here's the surprising part.

It's been 28 years since that time at Bricket Wood, but the bonds we forged remain as strong as ever. We still keep in touch, many of us. Some through social media, that inevitably turn into long threads of inside jokes, life updates, and the occasional photo of someone attempting to recreate one of our ridiculous outbound challenges in their office team-building days.

What began as a training program ended up being the foundation for lifelong friendships. I can still hear that French colleague's hilarious misquote and see the puzzled look on the Italian's face when we dared question his pizza expertise. Life at Bricket Wood had been a whirlwind—a glorious, messy, and unforgettable experience. I left with not only new knowledge and skills but also a treasure trove of memories, a heightened appreciation for cultural differences, and a firm belief that global teamwork often involves a lot of laughter and the occasional misunderstanding over pizza. And even after all these years, those memories and friendships continue to remind me how special that time was—proof that learning goes far beyond textbooks and into the heart of human connection.

CHAPTER 5

The Alchemy of Leadership: Rookie in Titan's World

I still remember my first day as a rookie Relationship Manager (RM) in the bustling world of institutional banking in Mumbai. The city itself was a beast—fast-paced, unforgiving, and relentless. And here I was, a young professional trying to make my mark among the titans of the banking industry. My role? To manage relationships with some of the biggest institutional clients, including corporations, government agencies, and banks. It sounded simple enough on paper, but in reality, it was anything but.

My desk was located on the senior management floor, a fact that both intimidated and thrilled me. It was an era when PCs were just becoming common, and emails had started replacing handwritten notes and memos. One of my earliest lessons came in the form of an embarrassing blunder.

I had left my computer unattended one evening, assuming that a blank screen meant it was shut down. The next morning, I arrived at work only to find an email sent from my mailbox to the Head of Financial Institutions Group (FIG) in Canada. The message was nonsense, but the damage was done. I was terrified. Who had sent it? Would I be reprimanded?

It wasn't until the end of the day that I gathered the courage to call the recipient in Canada. To my immense relief, he laughed it off as a prank, likely orchestrated by one of my senior colleagues. Though it turned out to be harmless, the incident taught me an invaluable lesson about digital security and accountability.

Meeting the Titans

One of the most fascinating aspects of my role was interacting with the top management of major Indian banks. These meetings were a masterclass in understanding the banking landscape, corporate strategies, and the future of financial services. Each meeting offered a unique perspective—some were focused on digitization, others on risk management, and a few on capturing emerging markets.

HSBC, with its global footprint, was a key player in the institutional banking space. Working alongside such a renowned organization added to the credibility of our offerings. During one of our client meetings, I vividly recall a discussion with a Chief General Manager (CGM) of a prominent Indian bank. He had a reputation for being unapproachable, yet our interaction turned out to be surprisingly engaging. He shared insights into how his bank was leveraging technology to streamline operations, a strategy that resonated deeply with our global expertise at HSBC.

Anecdotes that Shaped Me

Of course, not every interaction was smooth or conventional. I'll never forget the lunch meeting with an MD who ordered a Martini with Vodka – shaken not stirred. To my dismay, he expected me to enjoy the drink – à la James Bond. While the thought of reimbursement wasn't my primary concern, the idea of returning to the office reeking of alcohol left me uneasy. I politely sipped my drink, ensuring I drank as little as possible, and avoided everyone back at the office that day. Looking back, it's a memory that now makes me chuckle, but it also highlighted the peculiar challenges of navigating client relationships in an industry driven by personal connections.

Another unforgettable experience was the time I closed my first major deal. It was a complex transaction involving Cash letters service for a large nationalized Indian Bank. The process was grueling, requiring weeks of coordination with internal teams, credit analysts, and legal experts. When the deal finally came through, the sense of accomplishment was unparalleled. It wasn't just about the numbers; it was about the relationships I had built and the trust I had earned.

Challenges and Strategies

The role of an institutional RM came with its fair share of challenges. Understanding the intricate financial needs of large clients required not just technical knowledge but also emotional intelligence. Clients expected tailored solutions, and one-size-fits-all approaches simply wouldn't cut it. I spent countless hours studying market trends, analyzing credit reports, and brainstorming with colleagues to structure bespoke financial solutions.

Cross-selling was another critical aspect of my role. Promoting the bank's wide range of products required a deep understanding of each client's business model and long-term goals. For instance, a government agency might need cash management services, while a corporate client could be more interested in trade finance or foreign exchange solutions. The key was to position ourselves not just as service providers but as trusted advisors.

The Human Side of Banking

What often goes unnoticed in institutional banking is the human element. Behind every financial transaction and business deal were individuals with their own aspirations, fears, and pressures. Building relationships with these individuals was as much about empathy and trust as it was about numbers and spreadsheets.

One such relationship was with the CFO of a mid-sized corporation. Initially, he was skeptical about our offerings, given his past experiences with other banks. Over time, through consistent follow-ups, transparent communication, and a genuine effort to understand his company's needs, we turned his skepticism into confidence. Eventually, his company became one of our most loyal clients.

Looking back, my journey as a rookie RM in Mumbai's institutional banking sector was nothing short of transformative. It taught me resilience, adaptability, and the importance of staying grounded. Each challenge was an opportunity to learn, and each success reinforced my belief in the power of relationships.

The world of institutional banking is dynamic, demanding, and, at times, downright daunting. But it is also incredibly rewarding. The experiences I gained, the lessons I learned, and the people I met have left an indelible mark on my career and my life.

Even today, years later, I often find myself reminiscing about those early days. The mistakes I made, the victories I celebrated, and the relationships I built—all of them have shaped the professional I am today. If there's one thing I've learned, it's that in banking, as in life, it's the people who matter most.

ADMIN: Chaos in the Concrete Jungle

When I first joined the bank's management development program, I had visions of balance sheets, high-level client meetings, and the allure of institutional banking. What I didn't anticipate was being thrown into a role that had nothing to do with numbers and everything to do with holding together the chaos behind the scenes. This was my crash course in managing Mumbai's head office administration—a position that made me redefine what "banking" truly meant.

It all started innocuously enough. After a stint in institutional banking, I was told my next role would be in support services. My job? Managing infrastructure for the head office and seven branches across Mumbai, ensuring senior executives' accommodations ran smoothly, overseeing vehicles, coordinating guesthouses and holiday homes, liaising with municipalities, and keeping an eye on housekeeping and security. Essentially, I was expected to keep the entire non-financial apparatus of the bank running.

The resources under me were equally daunting: an officer, four assistants, 60 hamaals (office boys), and a mountain of expectations. My predecessor, Vivek, gave me a single day of handover before he was transferred to Bangalore. He explained the basics with the air of someone handing over a ticking time bomb.

"Expect calls 24/7," he said with a faint smirk. "And remember—everyone's crisis will always be more important than yours."

I brushed it off with optimism, but I quickly realized he wasn't exaggerating.

My first few weeks in the role were a whirlwind. It was like being dropped into a blizzard without any protective gear. Calls came in every minute, each more urgent than the last.

Maintenance issues, complaints about delayed services, requests from departments, executives—all needed to be solved immediately.

One day, while crossing the road to grab a quick lunch, someone shouted my name from across the street. I turned, only to see a BEST bus hurtling toward me. I narrowly avoided being crushed, but the irony wasn't lost on me: I was being asked about a request while dodging death.

Requests came from every corner. People would corner me in hallways, elevators, and even the restroom to discuss their grievances. I started keeping a pocket diary to jot down requests. By 10 a.m. each day, my to-do list was already page long. Forget time management theories; here, priorities were subjective. A leaking roof in a guesthouse was just as urgent as a missing AC remote in a senior manager's cabin.

Navigating the Chaos

The first few months were overwhelming, but they were also profoundly educational. I learned that managing operations was about more than tasks—it was about navigating relationships, dealing with egos, and staying resilient in the face of constant criticism.

One of the hardest lessons was realizing how transactional relationships could be. You could solve 99 problems for someone, but the one time you couldn't meet their expectations, your goodwill vanished. Even minor delays were met with frustration, regardless of the circumstances.

Senior management secretaries, for instance, held immense sway. These individuals could make or break your reputation with a single complaint. Managing them required a mix of tact, diplomacy, and impeccable follow-through.

Our team of hamaals added another layer of complexity. They were the unsung heroes of the bank, ensuring that tasks like delivering urgent letters, files, and setting up event spaces were handled seamlessly. Managing their schedules, addressing grievances, and ensuring they felt valued was a delicate balance. They looked to me for leadership, not just orders.

The other end of the spectrum involved dealing with municipalities, contractors, and vendors. Here, patience and negotiation skills were crucial.

Working in the administration department of a bank is like being the central nervous system of a living organism. You're privy to everything, from the grand decisions of the C-suite to the everyday quirks of juniors, peers, and even the spouses of executives. Add to this the interaction with public servants, political leaders, and ambitious businessmen, and you have a broad spectrum of personalities, behavior, and events to keep you on your toes. It's fascinating, inspiring, and at times, hilariously chaotic.

My 18-month stint in admin was eventful— where diplomacy, humor, and an uncanny knack for solving problems often saved the day.

Iron Lady with Golden Heart

Denise was the epitome of a no-nonsense manager, known across the organization as the unwavering head of support services for Western India. A seasoned professional, she had a reputation for toughness, which left many wondering if she was hands-on or simply a master delegator. Her stern demeanor masked any hint of softness, making her both respected and feared.

Administration was part of her domain, but Denise had a peculiar approach. She delegated the entirety of accountability and responsibility to the administration manager. "I don't care what you do or how you do it," she would often say, "just make sure there are no complaints." For many, this was a daunting mandate, especially in a thankless role like administration. It seemed Denise reserved her focus and energy for what she considered more critical support functions, such as back-office operations and remittances.

When I joined her team, I quickly learned that managing my relationship with Denise was a task in itself. Her unpredictability kept everyone on their toes. I decided to adopt a proactive approach, giving her daily updates on any potential issues before they could escalate. This strategy allowed me to safeguard my position and ensured she was never blindsided. Yet, no amount of preparation could truly prepare one for Denise.

One memorable instance stood out. I needed to request annual leave, but I dreaded the idea of approaching her. A colleague from the remittance department, privy to her mood swings, whispered one morning, "Denise seems to be in a good mood today. Maybe you should try now." Taking the advice to heart, I waited until mid-morning, after completing my daily updates. I mustered my courage and approached her desk.

Before I could even finish my sentence, Denise erupted. Her tone was sharp, her words cutting. "You think this is the time to talk about leave?" she barked, her voice echoing through the room. I stood there, stunned, wondering how I had misjudged the situation so badly. Later, I realized this was simply Denise being Denise—a mix of high expectations and an unpredictable temperament.

Interestingly, my reporting officer, a far more laid-back individual, avoided dealing with her altogether. He left the task of managing her moods and expectations squarely on my shoulders. It was exhausting, but, in hindsight, a valuable lesson in managing up.

As time passed, my perspective on Denise began to evolve. While her tough exterior made her seem impenetrable, glimpses of her humanity emerged. After I transitioned out of the administration role, our dynamic changed completely. Freed from the constant pressure of day-to-day interactions, we found common ground. Denise, surprisingly, was a warm, witty individual with a beautiful heart.

I'll never forget the first time I saw her laugh—really laugh. It was contagious and unguarded, shattering the image of the fearsome manager I had once tiptoed around. Denise taught me that leadership, even when tough, often conceals a deeper sense of care and commitment. Looking back, I realized she had been shaping me for challenges I hadn't yet imagined.

The Case of the Missing Car Keys

The drama unfolded late one Friday night. A senior executive, having indulged in a few drinks too many, called me in a panic.

"I've lost my car keys! I need the duplicate set immediately!" he slurred.

It was midnight. I lived 40 kilometers away from the office, and even by the most optimistic standards, retrieving the keys from the office and delivering them to him was going to take hours. Sensing the urgency in his voice, and also recognizing the alcohol-induced exaggeration, I decided to play along.

"Not a problem, sir," I said reassuringly. "I'll arrange for someone to leave for the office right now. He should reach you by dawn."

The line went silent. After a pause, he muttered, "Uh... you know what? Forget it. I'll figure it out."

The next morning, I went to the office, fetched the spare key, and handed it over to him. He looked sheepish. "Turns out the valet had the key all along," he mumbled, avoiding eye contact.

Lesson learnt: Always wait for sobriety to prevail.

The Air Conditioner that Couldn't Wait

It was a humid summer night when another C-suite executive called at 10 PM, distraught because his air conditioner had stopped working.

"Anil, can u arrange to fix this?" he politely asked as he had his guests (mother-in-law) staying with him.

The urgency in his tone made me feel like I was dealing with a tricky situation. Luckily, providence intervened. I remembered that one of our empaneled service agents lived nearby. A quick call later, he agreed to drop by the executive's house.

Within 10 minutes, the AC was back in action, and the chill was restored. The executive later called to thank me, a rare acknowledgment in the thankless world of admin.

Lesson learnt: Timing is everything, but a good network is even better.

Work Life Balance Lessons from a C Suit Executive

One of the more fascinating characters I dealt with was a senior executive known for his razor-sharp focus and incredible time management skills. He would call me at 8 AM sharp, often with a list of tasks for the day.

At first, I found it slightly annoying. But over time, I began to admire his discipline. His ability to prioritize, delegate, and follow up was unparalleled.

Observing him taught me the value of starting the day early and staying ahead of the curve. It wasn't just about being productive; it was about setting the tone for the rest of the day.

Lesson learnt: The early bird doesn't just catch the worm; it organizes the worm-catching committee.

The Great Car Allotment Saga

In our bank, executives promoted to a certain cadre were entitled to a company car. Usually, the vehicles were allotted from a pool of existing cars, but there was always a touch of drama involved.

One such instance involved three promotions but only two cars were available in the pool. This left me with no choice but to order a new car for the third executive. Using my discretion and past interactions, I decided who among the three would get the new car, having checked with each of them how urgent it was for them to get the car.

When the shiny new vehicle was delivered, the chosen executive was over the moon. The other two, while slightly envious, accepted it graciously.

Word of this decision spread quickly, and my reputation as a fair yet tactful administrator grew stronger.

Lesson learnt: Sometimes, it's not just about what you do but how you do it that makes all the difference.

Meeting with Municipal Commissioner

During my tenure, I had the privilege of meeting various dignitaries, including a municipal commissioner who left a lasting impression on me.

Unlike many who wield power with arrogance, he was polished and soft-spoken. His demeanor commanded respect without demanding it. Watching him handle a tense discussion with a blend of diplomacy and firmness was like attending a masterclass in leadership.

Lesson learnt: True power doesn't need to shout; it speaks softly and carries an undeniable weight.

The Business Agendas

If there's one group that kept me constantly on my toes, it was the businessmen who frequented our bank. Most were charming and outwardly friendly, but their motives were rarely altruistic.

One particular gentleman made it a point to invite me to every social event he hosted, from cocktail parties to his daughter's wedding. His goal was clear: to curry favor and gain access to the bank's decision-makers.

I learned to navigate these relationships with a balance of politeness and professional boundaries. It was a delicate dance—accepting goodwill without compromising integrity.

Lesson learnt: Not every handshake is a gesture of friendship; some come with strings attached.

Tact, Diplomacy, and the Art of Humor

Admin life often required more than just efficiency; it demanded tact and diplomacy, especially in delicate situations.

Humor, I found, was an invaluable tool in diffusing tension.

Once, an executive stormed into my office, fuming over a trivial delay in his request. "This is unacceptable!" he thundered.

I responded with mock seriousness, "Sir, I deeply apologize for not being omnipotent. I'll work on acquiring superpowers immediately."

He burst out laughing, and the matter was resolved in minutes.

Lesson learnt: A well-timed joke can often achieve what a detailed explanation cannot.

Building Relationships and Gaining Visibility

Despite its challenges, admin work offered a unique opportunity to build relationships across the hierarchy. Whether it was helping a junior with a personal request or coordinating with the spouses of executives for an event, every interaction added a layer to my network.

These connections not only made my job easier but also gave me visibility within the organization. Being the go-to person for solving problems earned me a reputation that went beyond my official role.

Lesson learnt: In the world of admin, relationships are your real capital.

A Thankless but Fulfilling Job

Admin work may not come with the glamour or recognition of other roles, but it has its rewards. The satisfaction of solving a problem, the lessons learned from observing diverse personalities, and the ability to influence outcomes in subtle ways make it a deeply fulfilling experience.

If I had to sum it up, I'd say this: Admin life is a mix of chaos and charm, a place where humor meets hard work, and where the small things you do often leave the biggest impact.

Lesson learnt: Even in a thankless job, the joy lies in knowing you made a difference.

As I look back on these anecdotes, I can't help but chuckle at the absurdity and brilliance of it all. From the case of the missing car keys to the AC crisis, each moment was a lesson in human behavior and problem-solving.

Admin life may not always be easy, but it's never dull. And that, I believe, is the best part of the job.

Battle of Wits

DD had joined as the admin officer a few weeks before I did. He was an ex-serviceman; he told me with pride. Smartly dressed, and full of energy, he appeared the perfect fit for the role of assisting me in the day-to-day functioning of the office. What struck me most about him was his leadership style—hands-on, and quick to adapt to any situation.

He loved holding a daily durbar with the sixty-odd hamaals who worked in our department. Every morning, they would gather around him, and he would assign them tasks based on their aptitude and experience. It was like watching a master strategist at work. The street-smart ones, the quick thinkers, were earmarked for firefighting errands, the sort of tasks that required rapid problem-solving and initiative. He knew how to delegate efficiently, bringing out the best in each individual.

Behind his charming exterior and boundless energy, there was a method to his madness. I noticed that Devi had a keen understanding of the senior management's requirements—getting cars serviced, maintenance of flats, organizing repairs, and dealing with building maintenance issues. He thrived outdoors and seemed to seize every opportunity to be out of the office during the day. It was almost as if he lived for the freedom of managing logistics from a distance, getting things done while remaining physically outside the constraints of an office.

However, as we worked together, I also discovered that there were aspects of his role that he seemed to avoid. Responsibilities such as inventory management, bills and accounting, and maintaining proper records were tasks he never seemed to neither have interest in or enough time for. While I was focused on reducing costs and increasing process efficiencies, DD appeared more comfortable in the operational side of things, managing people and taking care of "on-the-ground" activities.

Unjamming the Printer

One of the first challenges I faced involved renegotiating our vendor services and pricing. I believed that the company was being overcharged for many supplies, and I wanted to explore new options that would benefit the organization. As a result, I decided to change one of our key suppliers—the paper supplier. I found a new company that offered paper of better quality and faster delivery at a significantly lower price—50% cheaper, to be exact.

Resistance was palpable, especially from those accustomed to the old supplier. The print room, which was under my control, had a daily load of printing around 10,000 statements. Changing the paper supplier would certainly disrupt the flow of operations, but I was confident that the benefits would outweigh the risks. I decided to gradually phase in the new supplier by giving them 25% of the daily print load to start with.

It didn't take long before I started receiving late-night phone calls about problems with the new paper. The complaints were always the same: the paper quality was poor, the printing machines kept getting stuck, and the statements wouldn't be printed. Frustrating as it was, I refused to be deterred. Instead of switching back to the old supplier, I instructed the new paper vendor to be on standby at night, ready to handle any issues as they arose.

One night, just as expected, I received a call about the paper getting stuck. I told them to wait for my instructions. When I arrived at the print room, I brought the supplier's representative along. Together, we inspected the issue and found there was no real problem with the paper. The machine had been running fine all along, and production resumed without a hitch.

The following days saw the supplier's representative staying in the print room at night to ensure smooth operations. Slowly, the complaints faded away, and the machine ran without interruption. Over time, we shifted the entire print load to the new supplier, and I was able to secure substantial savings for the company. But I couldn't shake the feeling that some vested interests had been at play in the initial resistance to the new supplier. Nonetheless, my persistence had paid off.

A 1000 Km Test Drive

Another interesting episode occurred around the maintenance of company cars. DD had set up a contract with a local garage for the regular servicing and repairs of company vehicles. It was a necessary arrangement, given the number of cars executives used on a daily basis. However, many of the company's executives seemed to treat their cars with little regard for upkeep. The notion that the company would cover all maintenance costs led to a sense of entitlement. Cars were constantly being brought in for repairs, some of which seemed minor or even avoidable.

One day, an expatriate executive came to me requesting that his high-end car be checked for a fault and serviced before he went on leave for ten days. He insisted that the car should be in perfect condition before he left. I promptly arranged for the car to be taken to the garage for inspection.

To my surprise, I received a nasty email shortly afterward accusing me of impropriety. The executive had apparently noted down the car mileage before handing over his car for an issue. He informed that the car had been driven for a thousand kilometers during the time he was away—an unacceptable breach of protocol. The car was meant to remain stationary while the repairs were being carried out, but it had evidently been used, under the pretext of a test drive.

This incident marked the end of my relationship with the garage and, to a degree, with him. It became clear that the lack of oversight had resulted in several such instances going unchecked. His reluctance to confront his connections and address the issue head-on was troubling. The situation not only soured my relationship with him but also created a growing distrust between us.

The Hamaals and the Hawkers

The real test of my management skills, however, came when an unexpected challenge arose. All of a sudden, overnight, dozens of street hawkers appeared outside our office building, each with a valid license issued by the municipality. The building was a heritage site, owned by a foreign bank, and this created additional complications. The hawkers were creating a nuisance, blocking entrances, and disrupting the work environment.

I was tasked with evicting them, which required significant effort. I had to meet with the municipal commissioner to resolve the issue, and the process was more complex than I had anticipated. It took considerable time, resources, and diplomacy to finally clear the area.

During this period, the pressure was mounting, and my tactics—my ruthless efficiency in resolving issues—seemed to have drawn the ire of several parties. Even the hamaals, who had once respected my authority, began to complain about the way I was handling matters. It was only due to my old acquaintances that I was able to negotiate with the leader of their association to maintain order. Refusing to accept any favors or concessions, I managed to get the situation under control, albeit with a lot of effort.

In the midst of all this, I began receiving subtle threats, warning me to back off from my course of action. The pressure, both from within the company and from external sources, was immense. Yet, I remained resolute in my approach. I had faced adversity before, and this was no different.

A Lesson in Integrity

Not all moments were humorous. One of the most challenging decisions I faced was firing an office boy who forged my signature on a cash voucher. In the everyday rhythm of bank operations, peons often ran errands — delivering documents, collecting papers. For each trip, they were reimbursed through a simple cash voucher process: recommended by their reporting officer and authorized by me.

One afternoon, Sarita, our sharp-eyed teller supervisor, called. "Anil," she said, "There's a cash voucher here that appears to have your signature — but something feels off. Could you confirm if it's yours?"

I asked for the voucher to be sent across. One look was enough. It was not my signature. The strokes were unnatural, the alignment off. I hadn't signed this — it was a forgery.

On the other hand, it was just ₹20.

I reported it to HR. The investigation was swift. The peon who had submitted the voucher admitted to forging my signature. His explanation? The original voucher had been damaged in the rain, and the ink had smudged. Afraid it would get rejected, he copied my signature onto a new one — thinking no one would notice.

The consequence was decisive. He was dismissed from service. Not for the amount, but for the breach of trust— and the quiet moments where integrity is tested, not by grand gestures, but by tiny choices.

This was not a story about ₹20.

It was a story about the first crack in the foundation. A seemingly small act, left unaddressed, becomes a habit. And habits shape cultures.

That day, I was reminded that leadership must act — not based on value, but on values. Because when it comes to integrity, there is no such thing as a small compromise.

Always See the Bigger Picture

By the time my stint in support services ended, I had gained more than just operational experience. I had learned to manage competing demands, navigate human dynamics, and stay calm under relentless pressure.

I also gained a newfound appreciation for the invisible machinery that keeps organizations running. While the world focuses on the glamorous aspects of banking, it's the behind-the-scenes roles that ensure those moments of glamour are possible.

Looking back, I wouldn't trade this experience for anything. It shaped me as a leader, taught me resilience, and gave me stories that I'll carry for a lifetime. To anyone facing a role like this, my advice is simple: embrace the chaos. It's not just a test of your skills; it's a journey that will transform you in ways you never imagined.

A Vacation to Remember

Staying away from parents, summer vacations were cherished and eagerly awaited. Every year, we planned meticulously, combining time with family in New Delhi with the thrill of exploring a new destination. That year, our excitement soared as we finalized the details—Mumbai to New Delhi on the Rajdhani Express, followed by a journey to the enchanting hills of Darjeeling and Sikkim. The timing was impeccable, with my cousin's wedding in New Delhi allowing us to partake in the festivities before venturing into the mountains.

North Indian weddings are a spectacle to behold—a kaleidoscope of colors, laughter, and rituals. The celebrations were in full swing, with relatives gathered from far and wide. Our five-year-old son, Rohan, was particularly thrilled. He spent his time chasing after his older cousins and sneaking extra servings of sweets, his laughter blending seamlessly with the sounds of dhol and shehnai.

Then, calamity struck. A stray dog bit Rohan while he was playing outside. Though the wound was minor, the sight of the bite mark filled us with dread. We rushed him to a nearby clinic, where the doctor treated the wound and recommended a course of anti-rabies injections. These shots needed to follow a strict schedule, adding a layer of complexity to our carefully laid plans.

The first shot was administered immediately, and the next was due five days later, which meant that even as we packed for the hills, we had to strategize about managing Rohan's medical needs. Despite the disruption, our spirits remained high.

After three days of wedding festivities, we boarded the Guwahati Rajdhani Express, bound for Siliguri. The train was predictably delayed, arriving several hours behind schedule. By the time we stepped onto the platform in Siliguri, it was 3 PM—well past the time we had hoped to begin our drive to Darjeeling.

We hired an Omni van to take us up to the hills. The driver, cheerful and confident, suggested a shortcut that would save us an hour. Intrigued and eager to reach Darjeeling before nightfall, I agreed.

As the drive began, the beauty of the Himalayan foothills cast a spell on us. The narrow road twisted and turned, with hills rising steeply to our left and a deep valley to our right. The golden light of the setting sun bathed the landscape, creating an ethereal glow. We played music and allowed ourselves to relax, savoring the start of our adventure.

Then came the moment that would forever change our lives.

The driver, feeling perhaps too comfortable on the winding road, decided to change the cassette in the music player, steering with one hand. In the split second that his attention wavered, the van swerved slightly to the left, grazing the hillside. Startled, the driver overcorrected, jerking the steering wheel to the right.

The van tipped and began to roll.

The world turned upside down—literally and figuratively. The van tumbled down the slope, crashing through bushes and rocks. Inside, we clung to each other, shouting and bracing ourselves against the relentless jolts. It felt like an eternity, but in reality, the ordeal lasted only moments.

Abruptly, the van came to a halt. Silence descended, broken only by the sound of our breathing and the distant chirping of birds. The van had stopped rolling, caught between two sturdy tree trunks that jutted out from the slope like protective arms. Disoriented but alive, I asked, "Is everyone okay?"

One by one, voices emerged. My wife, my children, even the driver—all were shaken but unhurt. It felt like a miracle. I took a moment to gather my thoughts, then instructed the driver to honk the horn and flash the headlights to signal for help.

Before long, we heard voices calling out and saw beams of light from flashlights. Good Samaritans from passing vehicles had stopped to help. They reassured us that the van was stable and guided us as we crawled out, one by one. The climb back up to the road was difficult, but we made it, our relief palpable as we finally stood on solid ground.

Once everyone was safe, I went back down to retrieve our luggage. As night fell, the prospect of finding a new cab seemed grim. We were miles from Darjeeling, and the road was eerily deserted. After much pleading and offering double the fare, we managed to convince another driver to take us the rest of the way.

This time, I laid down strict instructions: no music, no distractions, and no speeding beyond 20 kilometers per hour. The driver nodded solemnly, clearly sensing the gravity of the situation.

Despite our precautions, the journey was fraught with tension. Halfway to Darjeeling, the car jolted suddenly as a tire burst. The vehicle swerved dangerously before the driver brought it to a stop. My nerves were on edge, but we pressed on, determined to reach our destination.

It was well past midnight when we finally arrived in Darjeeling. Exhausted and famished, we were greeted by another setback—the hotel had canceled our reservation due to our delayed arrival. The manager was unsympathetic, but after much pleading and a few tears from my wife, he relented, offering us his personal room and a couple of packets of Maggi for dinner.

The next morning, we visited a local hospital for a thorough check-up. To our dismay, the doctor discovered that our daughter had fractured her little finger during the accident. She received treatment, and we turned our attention to the next challenge: finding the second dose of Rohan's anti-rabies shot.

The search took us across the hill station, from one pharmacy to another. Finally, after hours of frustration, we found a clinic that stocked the vaccine. The ordeal consumed most of the day, leaving us drained but relieved.

Determined to salvage the trip, we spent the next few days exploring the beauty of Darjeeling. We visited its famous tea gardens, marveled at the views from Tiger Hill, and took a ride on the iconic toy train that chugged its way through the misty hills.

From Darjeeling, we traveled to Sikkim, where the tranquil beauty of the state rejuvenated our spirits. At Nathu La, we stood awestruck at the India-China border, the air heavy with the weight of history. The orchid farms, bursting with color, were a testament to nature's artistry. For a brief time, the trials of our journey faded into the background.

Yet, the memory of the accident lingered. I found myself pondering the forces at play that day. Was it sheer luck, divine intervention, or some combination of both that had saved us? I didn't know. All I knew was that we had come perilously close to tragedy and emerged with only minor injuries.

The vacation ended on a reflective note. Back in Mumbai, as I resumed work, life threw another surprise. The HR manager called me into his office to deliver unexpected news: As a part of the management program, I was being transferred to Bangalore to set up and manage the credit cards department. It was an opportunity that came with immense responsibility. In the past, such news might have unnerved me, but after surviving the harrowing events of our trip, I felt ready to take on any challenge.

That summer vacation remains etched in my memory—not just for the breathtaking sights and the joy of family, but for the profound lessons it taught me about resilience, gratitude, and the unpredictability of life. It reminded me of the fragility of existence and the strength of the human spirit to persevere against all odds.

Life, like a winding mountain road, is full of twists and turns. But with courage, faith, and a little bit of luck, we can navigate even the steepest climbs.

The End of My Admin Tenure

After 18 months of navigating these turbulent waters, my tenure as the admin officer came to an end. I had survived the many challenges thrown my way, some of which had seemed insurmountable at times. From managing DD's man-management style to renegotiating vendor contracts, to dealing with rogue garage owners and hawkers, it had been a rollercoaster ride.

In the end, the lessons I learnt were invaluable. The importance of building trust, of maintaining integrity in all dealings, and of standing firm in the face of adversity became clearer with every passing day. While my time with DD had been marked by disagreements and clashes of style, I emerged from the experience stronger, more capable, and far more prepared for the challenges that lay ahead.

CHAPTER 6

Bangalored

Banking, Babaji, and Beyond

It was a gloomy, rainy Mumbai morning when my phone rang, marking the beginning of one of the most transformative chapters of my life. Hong Kong Bank was rebranded as HSBC and was now expanding its credit card business. Bangalore was the new frontier. "We need you there," said the voice on the other end, "and you've got a week to relocate."

A week? That wasn't just short notice; it was a sprint. Amid packing boxes and hurried goodbyes, my friend Vivek, already stationed in Bangalore, quipped, "Looks like you're following me again!" Our bond, forged in the bustling chaos of New Delhi's offices, promised to make this transition smoother—or at least more entertaining.

First Impressions: Method to Madness

The move was swift, and before I knew it, I found myself at the iconic Manipal Centre off MG Road, Bangalore's beating heart. The office hummed with activity, and rightly so—our credit card base had surged to 50,000 customers, and the demands on my team were intense. As the Customer Service Manager, I led five customer service officers who handled an unending stream of complaints and queries, ranging from lost PINs to fee disputes. Adding to the mix were four merchant service officers and a team of seven collection agents who relied on me for operational and administrative support.

My counterpart, Pankaj, was an energetic and strategic leader overseeing credit card and merchant sales. We clicked instantly, and over time, our professional camaraderie evolved into a solid friendship. Every day, we visited key merchants across the city, tirelessly managing relationships and resolving service issues. If there's one thing Bangalore taught me early on, it was that service excellence wasn't optional—it was demanded, with urgency.

The Payment Conundrum

Merchant payments were a sensitive nerve. Every day, Sameer, our payments officer, would print and sign cashier's orders, which were then delivered across the city. This three-hour routine ended by noon, as merchants simply wouldn't tolerate delays. Their displeasure could escalate quickly, and the heat would land squarely on my shoulders.

During one of our casual pep talks, I discovered that Sameer was preparing for his MBA entrance exams, aspiring to join the prestigious Indian Institute of Management. Here was a young man juggling work pressures and academic dreams. "How's the preparation going?" I asked. He hesitated before admitting that the long hours were taking a toll.

An idea struck me. I offered him staggered hours: he could come in at 7 a.m., process payments by 10 a.m., and leave by 1 p.m. Sameer was overjoyed, and this small adjustment solved a major operational pain point. Months later, when he cracked the entrance exam and joined IIM Bangalore, I was as proud as a parent. Today, he's an economic adviser to a leading organization—a testament to what a little flexibility and belief can achieve.

Toothbrushing the POS Machine

In a bustling operation like ours, humor was never in short supply. One morning, a famous saree house called to report that their swipe machine hadn't been "serviced." Puzzled, I dug deeper. To my amazement, I learned that one of our acquiring officers had devised a unique way to delight merchants: he instructed delivery boys to carry toothbrushes and clean the swipe machines while delivering the cashier's orders. Ingenious? Yes. Unexpected? Absolutely. It was these small, thoughtful gestures that cemented our relationships with merchants, proving that going the extra mile didn't always require grand gestures.

However, not all technical issues could be solved with a toothbrush. One day, I received an urgent call from a top Sony dealer on Brigade Road. His POS machine had malfunctioned, and as a result, his payments were stuck in limbo. I rushed to his store, reviewed the paper trail, and assured him he'd have his payment by 10 a.m. the next day. It required special authorization from the head office and a sleepless night, but the promise was fulfilled. That merchant became one of our most loyal clients, often remarking, "This is the kind of service that earns trust."

Celebrity Card Fiasco

Not every day was smooth sailing. One of our officers excitedly informed me that he'd signed up a local celebrity for a credit card. Wanting to leave a lasting impression, he demonstrated the card's functionality at an ATM, withdrawing ₹100 and immediately depositing it back. What he didn't anticipate was that the system would classify it as a cash advance, triggering hefty fees and penalties. Months later, the celebrity stormed into our office, threatening legal action over the accumulating charges.

After a thorough investigation, we reversed the fees and apologized profusely. The officer, while sheepish, learned a valuable lesson about attention to detail. The incident became office folklore—a blend of humor and caution.

Bell Curve

By the end of my first year in Bangalore, I felt confident. Our team had achieved a significant turnaround, and I was optimistic about my appraisal. However, when the results were announced, I was downgraded by my counter-signing manager without any notice or explanation. My grievance was rejected on technical grounds – forced distribution to maintain the bell curve– leaving me frustrated and disillusioned.

But as they say, every setback is an opportunity in disguise. The incident caught the attention of the deputy head of credit cards, who began to notice my work. While I didn't realize it then, this visibility would play a pivotal role in my career trajectory.

Y2K: The Millennium Madness

As 1999 drew to a close, the world braced for Y2K—a potential technological apocalypse. Rumors of flights being grounded and systems crashing spread like wildfire. Our bank left nothing to chance. Staff were asked to remain on-site, and even families were invited to ensure everyone's peace of mind.

New Year's Eve was surreal. We huddled in the office, nervously watching as the data processing center ran year-end operations. Finally, at 6 a.m., the all-clear signal came through. Relief swept over us, followed by celebrations. For me, there was an additional reason to rejoice: I had been promoted to the next grade, a vindication after the earlier appraisal debacle.

Babaji and the Prophecies

Bangalore wasn't just about work; it had its share of mysticism. One evening, during a family wedding, my cousin introduced me to Babaji, a soothsayer with an uncanny reputation. As we walked to his house, he casually remarked, "Don't worry about the appraisal. You'll be transferred back to Mumbai soon."

Intrigued, I shared the encounter with Pankaj, who insisted on meeting Babaji. Over dinner, Babaji described Pankaj's appearance with startling accuracy and made a cryptic prediction: "Your life will transform in three years." True to his word, Babaji's prophecy came to pass. In August 2000, I was transferred back to Mumbai to handle special projects. To my shock, I was to report directly to the same counter-signing manager who had downgraded my appraisal. Life, it seemed, had a twisted sense of humor.

Reflections from Bangalore

My stint in Bangalore was a masterclass in leadership, resilience, and empathy. The challenges were many—resolving customer grievances, managing merchant expectations, and navigating internal politics—but each one shaped me into a more effective and compassionate leader.

The story of Sameer taught me the power of flexibility and nurturing talent. The toothbrush anecdote reinforced the value of small gestures in building relationships. And the appraisal debacle reminded me that recognition isn't always immediate but often comes when you least expect it.

Bangalore wasn't just a career milestone; it was a journey of growth and discovery. As I left the city, I carried with me not just a promotion but a treasure trove of lessons that continue to guide me in navigating life's unpredictable terrain.

The Home Coming - Breaking Barriers in Mumbai

Returning to Mumbai from Bangalore felt like entering a different orbit altogether. Bangalore had been my proving ground, a place where I built a reputation for reliability and operational excellence. But Mumbai, India's corporate nerve center, was where the real action was. It wasn't just a transfer; it was a leap into a faster, more competitive arena.

My new assignment in the Credit Card Division at Worli was nothing short of thrilling. The team had recently relocated to a sprawling, state-of-the-art office, and the buzz of activity was almost palpable. My task? To strategize an off-site merchant service model for regions where we didn't have branches.

The challenge was as exciting as it was daunting. With the credit card business expanding rapidly, we needed an operational blueprint that would ensure efficiency, customer satisfaction, and scalability—all without a physical presence in those regions. I relished the complexity of the task, confident that my experience had prepared me for this.

For two weeks, I immersed myself in research. I analyzed data, brainstormed solutions, and pored over market insights. What emerged was a comprehensive plan that mapped out how we could manage off-site merchant services seamlessly. It was detailed, efficient, and, if I may say so, rather brilliant.

The next logical step was to present it to the Business Head. That's when the real adventure began.

Mr. Elusive

The Business Head was a figure of great influence but even greater elusiveness. Getting on his calendar was akin to winning a lottery—something I quickly discovered after several attempts. His secretary, a harried yet unfailingly polite gatekeeper, assured me daily, "He's tied up today, but let's aim for tomorrow."

Tomorrow came and went, as did the next week. My frustration grew. I had a stellar plan ready for execution, but it was stuck in limbo. Determined, I decided to take matters into my own hands.

One morning, before the usual office bustle began, I stationed myself outside his cabin. The moment he arrived, I stepped in.

"Good morning, sir," I began, my voice steady. "I need just five minutes of your time."

He looked startled but waved me in. Before I could dive into my pitch, his phone rang. "Let's catch up at six," he said before rushing out.

At 6 PM, I was back. He was, predictably, on another call. I waited patiently, determined not to leave until I had his attention. After about twenty minutes, he finally glanced up, reviewed my plan briefly, and said, "Make these changes and bring it back."

What followed was a maddening cycle of revisions, resubmissions, and rescheduled meetings. Each time I returned with an updated version, he had more suggestions. On one occasion, as I waited outside his office, he emerged with a hurried, "My wife's waiting. Let's meet tomorrow morning." That morning, of course, never arrived.

My frustration was at its peak. The plan was gathering metaphorical cobwebs, and I was no closer to approval.

Then, during a late-night brainstorming session over coffee, inspiration struck.

I decided to approach a seasoned colleague known for his ability to navigate the labyrinth of corporate hierarchy. Over coffee, I shared my predicament—not as a complaint but as a frustrating puzzle that needed solving.

He listened intently, his eyes rolling with amusement, "Oh Ok," he said.

The next evening, I was sitting with the manager when our Cards Head came to his cabin and enquired what I was doing currently. And before the manager could even respond, he directed the manager that I should report to the Deputy Head of Cards.

Raj was something of a legend. A British gentleman of Indian origin, on an international secondment, he brought a wealth of experience and a no-nonsense approach to his role. His reputation as a credit card specialist preceded him, and his leadership style was admired across the organization.

"Can you come to my cabin?" he asked. "I've reviewed your project plan."

When I walked into his office, he greeted me with a firm handshake and wasted no time. "This plan is solid," he said. "From now on, you report directly to me. Let's get it rolled out immediately."

It was a moment of triumph. Within a fortnight, the off-site merchant service model was operational.

Working with a Mastermind

Under Raj's guidance, my responsibilities expanded. I now oversaw back-office operations, the 24/7 merchant service call center, and credit card customer services. The work was demanding, but the experience was transformative.

Raj was a master of precision. His British wit, coupled with an unwavering focus on results, made him both approachable and awe-inspiring. He had a unique ability to simplify complex problems, often with a touch of humor.

One afternoon, as we discussed a challenging situation, he leaned back and said, "You know, this is the kind of thing that separates the wheat from the chaff. I trust you'll sort it out."

His confidence in me was empowering, and I was determined not to let him down.

This chapter of my career was a masterclass in persistence, adaptability, and the power of strategic relationships. I learned that sometimes, when the front door remains closed, it's wise to find a side door—or create one.

It also taught me the value of patience and the importance of recognizing when to seek help. Raj's intervention wasn't just about the project; it was about having the right ally at the right time.

Looking back, I often laugh at the absurdity of my early attempts to secure a meeting with the Business Head.

Mumbai's ceaseless energy was the perfect backdrop for this transformative experience. The city demanded resilience, rewarded grit, and taught me to hustle like never before.

As I drove home one evening, reflecting on my performance, I felt a deep sense of accomplishment. This wasn't just about a job well done; it was about personal growth, resilience, and the art of making things happen.

It was a lesson I would carry with me for life.

Unlocking Productivity

The turn of the millennium brought with it exciting challenges in banking, and as the credit card business experienced rapid growth, so did the need to streamline processes. However, the manual personalization of credit cards was proving to be a bottleneck. Each delay chipped away at customer trust and satisfaction. It was taking up to a month from the time of application for customers to receive their cards—a glaring inefficiency that needed a swift and innovative turnaround.

When I took over the reins of this operation, my first move was to establish a service guarantee agreement with the vendor who had supplied our newly acquired automatic personalization machine. This agreement covered consumables, repairs, maintenance, and escalation protocols. With a vendor representative on standby for emergencies, I ensured the team had the necessary support to tackle any operational hiccups.

In just a few months, we achieved a 24-hour turnaround time for card personalization—an incredible leap forward. For a brief period, it felt like we had conquered the mountain. But success, as I learned, is often the beginning of new challenges.

A Lesson in Collaboration

With increased application volumes, we had to expand operations to two shifts. The bottleneck shifted from personalization to dispatch. Our personalized cards were handed over to Blue Dart, a logistics company, by 6 PM. While they were supporting us every time, our growing volume required a rethinking of the process.

I called for a meeting with Blue Dart's leadership team, including their VP, Balfour Manual. During the discussion, it was Satish, the youngest and most junior member in the room, and our assigned contact person for pickup, who confidently suggested rescheduling the pick-up time to 10 PM. This would allow us additional time to meet our production deadlines.

Satish's initiative and problem-solving mindset were impressive, but what stood out even more was the support he received from Balfour. As a leader, Balfour listened intently, trusted his team's abilities, and immediately approved the suggestion. His calm demeanor and willingness to empower a junior colleague reflected a leadership style that fostered trust and collaboration.

Over the next two years, despite growing volumes and occasional operational hurdles, Blue Dart consistently exceeded expectations. Even when unforeseen challenges like machine breakdowns arose, their team displayed unwavering commitment. Satish, in particular, went above and beyond, but this success was only possible because of the culture of accountability and mutual trust that Balfour nurtured within the organization. Today, Balfour serves as Blue Dart's Managing Director, a well-deserved recognition of his leadership ethos.

Reflecting on this partnership, I am reminded that great outcomes are not just about solving problems; they're about the culture that enables solutions. It raises the question: How can leaders inspire a shared sense of ownership and empower their teams to rise to any challenge?

From Chaos to Excellence

As we tackled one operational hurdle, another emerged. With personalization and delivery delays under control, the new monster on the horizon was rewards redemption. This non-core activity had become a headache, with redemption taking up to eight weeks. Complaints were piling up, along with losses, due to an increasing number of broken, damaged, or mismatched products.

To address this, I decided to simplify the catalogue by removing items prone to complaints, focusing instead on shopping vouchers from reputed stores. These were easier to manage and reconcile, significantly reducing the complexity of the process. To maintain oversight, I assigned one officer to manage the dispatch process, while a representative from an external service provider was stationed on-site.

Together, we streamlined operations, reducing turnaround times from eight weeks to just one week. A thunderous applause at a town hall meeting celebrated this achievement.

However, six months later, a discrepancy arose during reconciliation—a gap of ₹20,000 in vouchers. I assigned a senior officer to investigate discreetly. Her diligence revealed that the missing vouchers had been encashed. Suspicion pointed to the representative stationed on-site.

A review of security footage at a leading store confirmed our fears. The representative was indeed the culprit. While measures were taken to recover the loss and address the breach, it was a sobering reminder of the importance of vigilance, even in smooth operations.

This incident left me pondering: How do we maintain trust while ensuring robust checks and balances in our processes?

These three anecdotes from my career underscore valuable lessons in leadership and problem-solving. The credit card personalization challenge taught me the importance of establishing strong vendor relationships and leveraging technology to drive efficiency. The partnership with Blue Dart highlighted not just the power of collaboration but also the role of leadership in fostering a culture of trust, empowerment, and accountability. Balfour's willingness to support his team and Satish's ownership of the problem were critical to the success we achieved.

The rewards issue, on the other hand, underscored the need for vigilance and structured processes to prevent lapses, even when operations seem smooth.

In each case, the solutions were not merely operational but cultural. They were about fostering environments where people, systems, and partnerships worked seamlessly together. As I reflect on these experiences, I am left with a question: How can leaders ensure that their culture consistently inspires commitment, accountability, and vigilance across all levels?

Reflecting on these moments reminds me that every challenge is an opportunity to create systems, nurture talent, and build trust. The journey continues, with new lessons waiting to be learned.

Navigating Turbulence

It was a year of immense responsibility and transformation. I was entrusted with two critical assignments: setting up a new Customer Communication Unit and spearheading a major overhaul of our credit card operations. This entailed transitioning all operational activities to be centralized in-house. The task was far from straightforward—it required a complete review and redesign of existing processes while maintaining oversight and control within our team.

To rise to the challenge, I immersed myself in learning the intricacies of process design, time-motion studies, and control frameworks. My interactions with Suren, a composed and insightful leader, became pivotal. He played a crucial role in helping me understand the vast credit card ecosystem, spanning operations across the country. The work was intense, but the opportunity to contribute to such a transformative project made it deeply rewarding.

One evening, as I prepared to leave the office after a long day, my phone rang. It was the newly appointed Deputy Head of Credit Cards. His voice was sharp, carrying an urgency that left no room for delay.

"I need to see you. Now," he said.

Confused but compliant, I returned to the office and entered his cabin. His expression was stormy, his frustration evident. Without any preamble, a letter was tossed my way.

"This," he said, his voice rising, "is a customer response sent on behalf of the CEO. It's riddled with grammatical errors and fails to address the customer's complaint. How could you let this happen?"

I could feel the weight of his anger pressing down on me. Taking the letter, I scanned it quickly. A sense of disbelief set in—it wasn't written by me or my team. The reference number and tone indicated that it had originated from collections.

Maintaining my composure, I responded firmly but politely, "Sir, this letter wasn't drafted by me or anyone in my team. It's from the Collections Division."

Unconvinced and still visibly annoyed, he immediately called Hemant, the Head of Collections for Western India. Hemant entered the room, his curiosity evident. He handed him the letter and repeated his outburst.

Hemant examined the letter carefully. After a moment's pause, he responded in a measured tone, "Sir, this letter was approved by you."

The silence in the room was heavy and awkward. His frustration was palpable, but there was nothing more to be said. Feeling the tension, I excused myself and left the cabin.

Walking out into the night, I tried to shake off the lingering sense of injustice. It wasn't just about the misplaced anger; it was the assumption of guilt that left a sour taste.

While the Deputy Head had no further reason to criticize my work, I learned later on through Suren that he still harbored a grudge. Suren, with his characteristic tact and clarity, took the matter up. Speaking directly to him, he said, "We all know Anil's capabilities. His contributions have been exceptional, and his writing is outstanding. This shouldn't be about past grievances. We need to focus on his achievements and the value he brings to the team."

Suren's firm yet fair intervention put an end to the lingering negativity. While I wasn't directly involved in the conversation, I was deeply grateful for his leadership and sense of justice. It was a reminder of how a true leader prioritizes merit over bias and fosters harmony within the team.

Reflecting on this episode, I learned the importance of maintaining composure in the face of unwarranted criticism and the value of having allies who stand by what is right. It reinforced the idea that professionalism isn't just about competence; it's also about navigating interpersonal dynamics with grace and integrity.

As I look back, one question continues to resonate: How do we ensure that our professional judgments and actions remain free from bias, even when faced with personal frustrations?

CHAPTER 7

Stepping Up: New Challenges, New Triumphs

The Power of Big, Hairy, Audacious Goals

Restructuring was the word of the hour. The winds of change swept through our organization, and with it came a recalibration of priorities. Credit cards had been our core strength, a business we had nurtured with remarkable success, seeing a robust growth trajectory over the years. However, the horizon expanded: personal loans and home loans now joined the fold, reshaping our division into "Retail Assets."

The market was ripe with opportunity and challenge. New players were entering the fray, bringing innovation and competitive urgency. Amidst this transformation, Puneet arrived—a young, dynamic leader with the kind of charisma that could light up a room. His prior successes in the custody business and corporate banking had made waves, and his new role as Business Head for Retail Assets signaled a fresh, ambitious era.

Just days after Puneet's appointment, I had the privilege of receiving the CEO's Recognition Award at a town hall. It was a humbling moment that coincided with a palpable shift in the atmosphere. Over the following weeks, Puneet's leadership injected a renewed vigor into the team, culminating in the launch of an ambitious program that would soon become a defining chapter in our journey: Project 239.

239 - Unveiling the Dream

The unveiling of Project 239 at Aamby Valley was a spectacle of energy and optimism. All teams, from sales to support functions like credit underwriting, compliance, back-office operations, customer service, HR, and legal, came together under one roof. Puneet, with his characteristic flair, announced the BHAG (Big Hairy Audacious Goal) for the year:

- 2 million credit cards,
- ₹3 billion in personal loans per month, and
- 9% yield on the mortgage business.

The room buzzed with excitement. The enormity of the task ahead was clear—it was a leap from 1.1 million to 2 million credit cards in a year, and from ₹1 billion to ₹3 billion per month in personal loans disbursal. Similarly, the mortgage business yield was targeted to increase from 7.8% to 9%. Yet Puneet's confidence was infectious. He urged us to make the impossible possible, rallying us around the vision.

The year that followed was one of relentless focus and unyielding effort. Achieving the audacious goals meant functioning with the precision of a factory assembly line. Daily run rates became our mantra, turnaround times were sacrosanct, and every team member—from the front-line sales force to back-office staff—knew their role in the larger scheme.

Adding over a million accounts in a year required unparalleled coordination. A team of trainers emerged from within our ranks, traveling across the country to coach and upskill 7,000 feet-on-street (FOS) employees. High turnover among FOS staff was a given, but the commitment to training ensured that every new recruit hit the ground running.

Puneet's leadership was pivotal, but he was far from a solo act. Dheeraj, RSR and Sachin – all recent additions to the Retail

Assets team. While Dheeraj managed personal loan and credit card sales, RSR and Sachin managed regional mortgages sales. They brought their own distinct styles to the table. RSR was a popular people's manager, Sachin was a strategist, while Dheeraj was a master motivator who could electrify a room. Together, they complemented Puneet's visionary approach, creating a leadership trifecta that inspired confidence and results.

Every Monday morning, crisp and incisive meetings with function heads became the nerve center of our operations. Each department played its part in the symphony:

- The application processing team captured data with speed and precision.
- Underwriting meticulously reviewed each applicant to ensure adherence to the criteria.
- Personalization ensured that dispatches were timely and error-free.
- Finance tracked run rates and managed service provider payments without delay.

Puneet orchestrated this complex ensemble like a maestro, ensuring that every note resonated with clarity and purpose.

The journey was not without its challenges. Pressure mounted as the months rolled by, and skepticism from within and outside the organization lingered. Could we truly hit such lofty targets? Was it wise to stretch resources so thin?

But we persevered. Distribution networks expanded, and sales teams spread out across the country. Every day, we aimed to add 3,000 new credit card accounts. It was a humongous task, but the sheer grit and determination of the team were unmatched.

By the end of the year, Project 239 had achieved the unthinkable. We surpassed the targets, silencing the naysayers and proving that with the right mindset, even the most audacious goals are within reach.

The success of Project 239 called for a celebration befitting the magnitude of our achievement. The leadership team, along with key contributors, embarked on a trip to Greece—a well-deserved moment of reflection and camaraderie. As we stood on the shores of the Aegean Sea, basking in the glow of our collective success, I couldn't help but marvel at what we had accomplished.

It wasn't just about the numbers. It was about the journey—the relentless focus, the camaraderie, and the belief that audacious dreams could be turned into reality.

In the end, Project 239 was a testament to the power of ambition, leadership, and teamwork. It pushed us to our limits and beyond, proving that those who dare to dream big are the ones who ultimately win.

Question: When was the last time you dared to set a goal so big, so audacious, that it scared you—and yet, you pursued it with everything you had?

Friends for Life: Building Lifelong Connections in a Corporate World

In the labyrinth of corporate offices, where every cubicle holds a story and every meeting room a challenge, it's rare to find friendships that transcend the transactional. My cubicle, positioned strategically opposite Puneet's cabin, became a focal point for such connections. Puneet, with his towering reputation for excellence and exacting standards, inspired a mix of respect and fear. His always-open door symbolized transparency, yet it reminded us all of his watchful eye.

Situated right at the office entrance, my cubicle turned me into the unofficial gatekeeper. Arriving early each day, I became the first point of contact for many visitors. It was here that I met four remarkable individuals—Sachin, Sri, Sameer, and Sid—whose first steps into my orbit began friendships that have lasted a lifetime.

Sachin: The Brilliant Humanitarian

Sachin's entry into our office was understated, yet his presence soon became impossible to ignore. He joined as the strategy head for retail assets, a critical role requiring sharp intellect and a nuanced understanding of the business. My first interaction with him was brief—a casual conversation by the entrance where he had come to meet Puneet. What struck me was his calm demeanor, free of the arrogance that often accompanies high achievers.

Over time, I learned more about Sachin's background. A top talent from Jamnalal Bajaj Institute of Management Studies, he had already established a formidable reputation in the banking industry. But what set him apart was his simplicity and focus on substance over style. While others were quick to flaunt their credentials, Sachin preferred to let his work speak for itself.

As our professional paths crossed, I discovered that Sachin was more than just a strategist. He had a remarkable ability to distill complex problems into actionable solutions, always keeping the larger picture in mind. But what truly made him exceptional was his empathy. Whether it was mentoring junior colleagues or lending an ear to a troubled peer, Sachin was always there, quietly making a difference.

Our bond grew deeper as we shared discussions about work, life, and aspirations. Sachin's unwavering integrity and humility left an indelible mark on me, reminding me that true greatness often comes wrapped in modesty.

Srikumar: The Charming Oracle

Sri joined the marketing unit with a splash of charisma that lit up the office. Fair-skinned, with sharp features and an air of confidence, he exuded an effortless charm that drew people to him. Yet, it wasn't just his appearance that caught my attention—it was his energy. Sri had the rare ability to inspire trust and warmth in everyone he met.

Our first conversation happened when he came to meet Puneet. Something clicked immediately, and we moved from formal introductions to a candid exchange of ideas. Sri was disciplined, ambitious, and incredibly passionate about his work. He carried himself with a quiet assurance, and his enthusiasm for every task, no matter how small, was infectious.

Sri wasn't just a marketer; he was a visionary. He had an uncanny ability to predict market trends and craft strategies that were both innovative and practical. Whether it was launching a new product or managing a crisis, Sri always seemed to be one step ahead.

Our friendship deepened over time, fueled by shared interests and mutual respect. I admired his ability to balance his professional drive with a genuine concern for people. Sri often spoke about his fitness routines, a reflection of his discipline, and his love for travel, which added a unique perspective to our conversations. In a world that often prioritizes results over relationships, Sri taught me the value of infusing humanity into every interaction.

Sameer: Our Legal Shield

Sameer's journey into my life began with a simple gesture—a cup of coffee. He had recently joined the legal team and was waiting to meet Puneet, who was caught up in a meeting. Spotting his unfamiliar face, I invited him to the cafeteria, where we struck up a conversation. What started as a casual chat about work turned into a fascinating exchange about life, challenges, and opportunities.

Sameer quickly established himself as a cornerstone of the legal department. Unlike many legal professionals who strictly interpret the rulebook, Sameer had a gift for balancing compliance with business needs. He didn't just say what couldn't be done; he focused on finding ways to make things happen. His pragmatic approach and ability to offer actionable solutions made him an invaluable asset to the organization.

Our professional collaboration deepened as I worked closely with him in my capacity as a nodal officer. I often marveled at his sharp intellect and quick thinking, especially in high-pressure situations. Yet, what truly set Sameer apart was his humility. Despite his impressive credentials and undeniable talent, he remained approachable and grounded.

Over countless projects and late-night discussions, we forged a bond that extended beyond work. Sameer's insights, whether about legal intricacies or life in general, were always thoughtful and enlightening. His ability to navigate complex situations with grace and humor made him not just a colleague but a trusted confidant.

Sid Singh: The Handsome Trailblazer

Sid's entry into our office was as unexpected as it was impactful. One morning, as I was settling into my routine, a young man walked in, exuding confidence and charm. Fair-skinned and strikingly handsome, Sid carried himself with an effortless aura that was impossible to ignore. As was my habit, I greeted him warmly, offered him a seat in the cubicle behind mine, and inquired about his purpose.

Sid told me that he had joined our Merchant Acquiring team. This revelation immediately raised questions because we had recently divested our Merchant Acquiring Business. Since the Business Head was not in office, unsure of how to proceed, I informed Puneet, who promptly called Sid into his office.

Puneet, in his characteristic composed manner, made Sid feel at ease before addressing the situation. He explained the organizational changes and assured Sid that his expertise would not go to waste. True to his word, Puneet ensured that Sid was placed in a role that matched his capabilities.

Sid didn't just adapt—he thrived. His performance earned him recognition and an international posting in Hong Kong. Today, he is a CEO in the United States, a testament to his resilience, adaptability, and the faith Puneet placed in him. Sid's journey reinforced my belief in the power of second chances and the importance of leadership that nurtures talent.

Suren: A Kindred Spirit

Suren - my partner in crime since the dawn of the millennium! We bonded over our shared struggles in the same function, and when I got transferred to his hometown Mumbai in 2000, our friendship was cemented. Unlike Sachin, Sri, Sameer and Sid, whom I met as head of the welcoming committee for newbies at HSBC - (talk about pressure!) Suren and I had a more conventional meet-cute.

Suren exuded a kind of simplicity and focus that made him a natural leader—one who led by example rather than decree. Suren became more than a professional peer; he became my guide, my sounding board, and, eventually, my friend. We navigated the complexities of credit card operations together, learning as we went. While I brought energy and strategic thinking to the table, Suren contributed his in-depth knowledge of banking practices and procedures. His knack for dissecting problems with precision was invaluable, and I marveled at how effortlessly he made complex processes seem manageable.

Beyond the workplace, Suren introduced me to the heart of Mumbai. He knew every nook and cranny of the city, from the best lunch spots near Dadar Matunga to shortcuts that helped us avoid the ever-present traffic snarls. Lunchtime conversations with him were a mix of work and philosophy. Suren would speak about the importance of loyalty, humility, and the power of staying grounded—lessons that resonated deeply with me.

The Art of Connection

These friendships didn't arise from grand gestures but from simple, authentic interactions—a casual chat, an offer of coffee, or a helping hand. What united these individuals was their exceptional character, their ability to inspire trust, and their commitment to excellence.

In a corporate world dominated by targets and deadlines, it's easy to overlook the human element. But my experiences with them taught me that relationships are the true currency of life. These connections enriched my personal and professional journey, offering lessons in humility, resilience, and the power of genuine engagement.

Looking back, I often wonder: What made our partnership so seamless? Was it the shared sense of responsibility? More importantly, in a world increasingly driven by personal ambition, how often do we take a moment to prioritize collaboration over competition?

I realize that these friendships were no accident. They were nurtured through curiosity, mutual respect, and a willingness to go beyond the immediate demands of work. Suren's simplicity, Sachin's humility, Sri's charisma, Sameer's pragmatism, and Sid's resilience each left a lasting impression on me, shaping my perspective on life and leadership.

In the fast-paced world we live in, it's easy to get caught up in the grind and forget to pause and connect. But as these stories show, the greatest rewards often come from the simplest acts of kindness and curiosity.

How often do we take the time to truly connect with the people we encounter every day? Could a single moment of genuine engagement lead to a friendship that lasts a lifetime?

Going the Extra 400 Miles

Puneet had a flair in the way he did things, often with a touch of elegance and panache. Among his many quips, one line had gained legendary status: "Niall only knows Dheeraj and Anil!" The fact that our CEO was indeed familiar with my name, I dismissed it as playful exaggeration, but it had the unintended effect of setting certain expectations. Being in the good graces of the top brass came with an unwritten job description: any irate customer who dared bypass the usual channels to escalate directly to the CEO or Personal Banking Head would inevitably find themselves redirected to me. My role, unofficially, was to "make it disappear."

One otherwise quiet afternoon, the Head of Personal Banking called Puneet, who wasted no time in directing me to handle an escalating complaint from a UK-based Premier customer. "It's urgent," he added, before abruptly hanging up, leaving me to piece together what was clearly going to be a tricky case.

I hung up, mentally preparing myself for what would likely be a diplomatic minefield. I called the customer, a man whose clipped British accent was tinged with a now unmistakable tone of frustration. As he narrated his ordeal, the pieces of the puzzle began to fall into place.

He had lost his credit card and, understandably, called the call center to report it. The twist? He couldn't recall the card number, so the well-meaning agent decided to play it safe and block all his cards—credit and debit alike. While this move may have looked prudent on paper, in reality, it left the customer stranded. No credit card, no debit card, and consequently, no access to his bank account. To make matters worse, he was in a foreign country, miles away from home.

"Look," he said, his tone exasperated but restrained, "I just need cash to survive the next couple of days. The cards can take their sweet time getting to me."

"How much cash would you need?" I asked.

"₹10,000 should suffice," he replied.

Fate, in its peculiar way, had already intervened. Coincidentally, I was set to take my communication unit to Goa for an offsite that very evening. An idea sparked in my mind—a crazy one, but one that just might work.

I hung up the call and got to work. Exceptional approval to debit the customer's account? Check. Cash withdrawal? Check. A neatly drafted authority letter for his signature? Check. By the time we boarded our 5 PM flight, I had ₹10,000 in cash tucked safely into an envelope, along with the requisite paperwork.

Once we landed in Goa, I ensured my team was settled in at the hotel before setting off on my impromptu mission. The customer was staying in a resort that, as luck would have it, was 40 kilometers away. Undeterred, I hired a cab and braced myself for the long drive, marveling at how a career in banking could sometimes feel like the plot of a spy thriller.

When I finally reached the resort, it was well past 8 PM. The customer greeted me with equal parts disbelief and gratitude. "I can't believe the bank sent someone all the way here," he said, shaking his head.

I handed him the envelope, had him sign the authority letter, and reassured him that his replacement cards were already in process. "We're the world's local bank," I said with a smile, quoting our tagline.

It was almost 10 PM by the time I returned to the hotel, physically exhausted but strangely exhilarated. I sent a quick update to Nick, our Personal Banking Head, summarizing the day's events. His response came almost immediately: "Fantastic work! Truly going the extra mile—400 miles, to be precise."

The team found the entire episode hilarious. Over dinner, they teased me about being the bank's unofficial "mobile ATM" and debated whether we should add "courier service" to our portfolio of offerings.

Looking back, the incident was emblematic of the balancing act that defined my career. On one hand, the effort reinforced my reputation as someone who would stop at nothing to resolve a customer's problem. On the other, it raised the bar for what others expected of me, setting a precedent that would be difficult, and occasionally exhausting, to maintain.

As for the customer, I wonder what he tells people about that evening in Goa. Does he laugh at the absurdity of it all, or does he recount it as a testament to customer service at its finest?

And then there's the broader question that lingers in my mind: where do we draw the line between going the extra mile and going too far?

A Jolt of Joy

The office was a maze of chatter and clattering keyboards, but I was focused on one thing: the appraisal meeting with Puneet. As a senior leader, I had witnessed his no-nonsense approach firsthand. He was a taskmaster—someone who never condoned failure, expected solutions rather than just problems, and demanded only the highest standards from everyone. He would often quip, "I hate your job, but I love the way you do it." There was something about that line that always stayed with me. It was a mix of admiration for how I executed my duties and the relentless demand for excellence that Puneet embodied.

The appraisal season was always a charged atmosphere in the office, and this time, it was my turn to present the work I'd done over the past year. I had compiled my records, achievements, and a string of accolades into a hefty four-page document, ready to impress him. I was all set for the 1-1 meeting, scheduled at 5 p.m., filled with anticipation and confidence. However, I found his glass cabin door closed. It was unusual—his cabin was rarely shut unless he was in a critical meeting. I waited. And waited.

As the clock ticked past the appointed hour, I approached his secretary, who was just as unaware of him having any other meeting. I waited some more. By 6 p.m., I could see him walking out of his office.

Puneet didn't even glance in my direction. He left.

Dejected, I packed up my things and headed home. It was a frustrating end to an otherwise productive week, but I told myself that Monday would be a new day, and I'd have the opportunity to present my work.

When I walked into the office on Monday morning, Puneet was already there. The first thing he said after the morning meeting was to call me into his cabin. There was no mention of the missed appraisal. "Puneet, we were supposed to meet for the appraisal on Friday," I ventured, unsure how to approach the situation.

Yes, why didn't you turn up?" The tone was sharp, and I found myself fumbling for words. "Well, your cabin door was closed, and I checked with your secretary..." I stammered. Before I could finish, he snapped and said, "If you're given a time slot, you must show up on time. Don't assume anything!"

I was stunned. Came back to my desk. But I had little time to process it before his secretary called me again that evening. "Boss wants you for the appraisal NOW."

At that moment, I grabbed my papers, barely able to contain my nerves, and rushed into his cabin. This was my moment to showcase everything I had done, all the hard work, the hours I'd put in, and the results I had delivered. But Puneet had something else in mind.

He asked me to close the door and take a seat. I carefully placed my four-page appraisal sheet in front of him, feeling proud of my accomplishments. Puneet didn't even glance at the papers. Instead, he gently pushed them towards me and said, "Okay I'm listening. Tell me."

I was blank. Puneet, sensing the tension, gestured for me to have a sip of water, and said, "Explain to me your achievements as if this is an elevator pitch."

I froze. I couldn't form a sentence. My mind raced, but the words wouldn't come.

Seeing my struggle, Puneet simply watched. It was as though he knew exactly what was going through my head. Slowly, I regained my composure, and with effort, I listed out the top three items I'd accomplished over the year, in bullet points. Just three.

"That's wonderful, Anil," Puneet said with a hint of approval in his voice. "That's what I wanted you to realize and understand. As you rise higher in the hierarchy, brevity is the need of the hour. Do you think Niall would have listed his 50 pages of achievements? No. I'm fully aware of what you've contributed this year. Keep up the excellent work. I'm proud of you."

I sat there, taken aback.

That was Puneet. He never let me off easy, but he also never failed to push me in the right direction.

It was a lesson I would carry with me throughout my career—whether in leadership or communication. The need for brevity, focus, and the ability to highlight the core elements of success, rather than getting bogged down by details, was essential.

Looking back, I realize the lesson was far greater than just how to manage performance appraisals. It was a lesson in resilience, in understanding the expectations of leadership, and in not being afraid to fail, even in public.

Puneet's approach, though tough, was rooted in a desire for growth and excellence.

Have you ever been caught in a situation where you prepared extensively for something, only to realize that the essence of the matter was far simpler than you had imagined?

A Customer Who Took "Queries" to a New Level

There are customers who call with complaints, and then there are those who make their complaints an academic pursuit. I encountered one such character, who we'll call The Researcher. This customer didn't just dispute charges on his credit card. Oh no, he turned it into a study of credit card charges and banking policy that would rival any university thesis.

It started innocently enough—a call about late payment fees and revolving interest charges. However, this customer was not content with a simple explanation. He wanted it all: detailed breakdowns of our charges, the exact formula behind them, and references to specific clauses in our terms and conditions. He insisted on written responses, which, as you can imagine, wasn't just an extra step for the customer service team, it was a full-on research project.

For months, he called daily, speaking to random representatives, each of whom would give the same answer. Yet, every time he responded with the same demand: "Other banks explain this better. Why can't you do the same?" He wasn't just venting frustration. He was collecting data. After one particularly long exchange, I found out that he was writing a book on credit card charges, citing examples from various banks, including ours.

It seemed endless. Every time we referred him to the terms and conditions; he'd counter with a pointed remark about how other institutions handled it differently. No matter how much we explained, it wasn't enough. This was no longer about getting his issue resolved; it was a matter of principle, a mission to expose the "truth" behind credit card fees.

I couldn't help but admire his persistence. His level of detail was unmatched, and if there were an award for Most Persistent Customer, he would have taken the trophy home every year. In the end, after countless back-and-froths, he received his answers and likely added a new chapter to his book. I, on the other hand, learned an important lesson in customer persistence and the importance of clarity in communication.

The Case of the Vanishing Papers

If ever there was a case that made me appreciate the phrase "under promise, over deliver," it was the case of the missing house documents. A customer, furious and nearly shouting, stormed into the bank claiming we were holding onto his house documents despite him having repaid his loan. He needed the papers to sell his flat. So, the question was: Why hadn't we returned them?

I quickly took the customer's details and promised to resolve the issue within a week. As it turned out, things were not as straightforward as they seemed. The customer had purchased the flat from someone who had borrowed money from another bank. When our representative had processed the payment for the flat, he was told that the documents had already been handed over by the seller's bank. No one double-checked the paperwork. In fact, no one seemed to care enough to follow up.

After digging further, I found that the documents were, in fact, lost—washed away in floods in Chennai years ago. The other bank's representative admitted as much, but they agreed to arrange for a duplicate set and send us an undertaking about future liabilities.

The customer's frustration turned to relief, and my team and I learned a valuable lesson in accountability. The case revealed the importance of ensuring ownership of every step in the process—something that, unfortunately, hadn't been handled well from the beginning.

Both of these experiences taught me crucial lessons about customer service. The Researcher's unyielding quest for answers emphasized the value of clear, concise, and transparent communication. On the other hand, the Missing Documents case drove home the need for accountability at every stage of a process. But here's the big question: In a world where time is of the essence, how far are we willing to go to provide customers with the answers they seek, even when the demands seem unreasonable? Do we risk losing the human touch in the pursuit of efficiency?

Champion of the Grievance Games

It was one of those days at the call center, where the hum of the phone lines almost made you question if there was ever truly silence in this world. Between the complaints, claims, and endless requests for compensation, every new call was a chance to either save the day or test your patience. But one customer was different. He was a legend of sorts—his name might as well have been etched into the walls of the call center.

This wasn't your typical customer. Oh no, this was the customer who insisted on everything. He was an expert in the art of complaint, a maestro of minor grievances. It was as though he had an unspoken rule book that everyone in the call center had memorized over time. From the head of the call center to the TSRs, everyone knew him by his issues. And, of course, everyone knew about his insistence on written responses and compensation claims.

It wasn't enough that he had his fingers in the proverbial pie of multiple banks. The man was practically a compensation connoisseur—someone who could sniff out an error from miles away and demand compensation with the precision of a seasoned negotiator. It turns out, he wasn't just calling us for fun; he had successfully garnered compensation from several other institutions as well. I guess you could say he was a bit of a professional customer.

But this story really picks up when he started calling about the ATM guard.

Ah, the ATM guard. Not the first figure you'd think of when you think of security breaches. But apparently, to our esteemed customer, this particular guard had committed the ultimate sin. While he was entering his PIN, the guard—who, by the very nature of his job, stood at a distance—wasn't looking at him with the attention he so deserved. This, in the customer's mind, was a security breach. The violation was so egregious that it warranted compensation. Yes, you read that right. Compensation for being snooped at by an ATM guard. Naturally, this all made its way up to the CEO's office. The customer had one simple demand: speak to the CEO, or nothing would satisfy him. After all, why should an ATM guard's lack of focus on him not be addressed by the topmost authority?

Now, this wasn't the first time someone had complained to the CEO's office, but it was certainly one of the more... peculiar ones. Florence, the very capable and ever-so-wise colleague, informed me that I would be the lucky one to handle this case. I must say, I wasn't thrilled. Talking to someone who seemed to believe that every inconvenience in life warranted monetary compensation was not how I had imagined my afternoon.

After some back-and-forth, I finally got him to agree to meet. I had to introduce myself as the "Nodal Officer"—a title that, in hindsight, may have sounded more important than it actually was. To my surprise, he showed up on time. He was impeccably dressed, as polished as a movie star at a premiere, and his demeanor was that of someone who had seen the world and knew how to command respect. Calm, composed, and definitely not someone to be trifled with. I mean, who else could demand compensation for a guard not looking at them during an ATM transaction?

We sat down, and I began my best attempt at diplomacy. I explained the situation with the ATM guard. The protocol was clear—our guards were to remain outside the ATM at a safe distance to respect customer privacy. We had made it abundantly clear to our team that the guards were not supposed to be hovering over the customers or peeking inside the machines. The man listened attentively, nodding along as if he were contemplating the fate of the universe.

But then came the clincher: "And as for compensation, well, we cannot provide any as per company policy."

There was a slight pause. It was the kind of pause where you could practically feel the pressure in the air. But the customer, ever composed, simply nodded again, as if he'd heard this response a thousand times before. He didn't even flinch. And just like that, he didn't push any further. The message was clear: No compensation, no matter how hard he tried. I quickly called Florence to inform her of our discussion and shared a draft response on behalf of the CEO.

The matter, at least for us, was done and dusted. The call center could go back to its regularly scheduled programming of complaints and claims.

However, I must admit—after the meeting, I found myself a little curious. What kind of person could take something so trivial and turn it into a quest for compensation? Was he really out to get us, or was this just his way of ensuring that every inconvenience in life was met with some form of retribution? Was this man simply an eccentric customer, or a product of a society that had begun to demand answers for the smallest of perceived wrongs?

Reflecting on the experience, I couldn't help but wonder: In a world that often seems driven by demands and complaints, where do we draw the line between genuine grievances and the desire for rewards, even when the issue might be, let's face it, totally ridiculous?

And perhaps, the bigger question remains: Are we, as a society, growing more sensitive to every slight, or are we simply getting better at spotting opportunities for a little extra something for our trouble?

The Promotion That Never Came

It was just another routine fire drill at the bank, the kind we did regularly as part of our safety protocol. The building was evacuated, and we gathered at the rally point, ready for the drill to conclude. But then, out of nowhere, Puneet, a senior leader, walked over to me with a grin and patted me on the shoulder.

"A new city, a new challenge: get ready for the next step in your career," he said.

I was rooted to the spot, trying to process what he had just told me. A promotion? To say I was stunned would be an understatement. The excitement didn't fully register until days later, when the full picture began to emerge.

Puneet was moving to head Commercial Banking, and Dheeraj, his successor, who was hitherto heading Retail Assets Sales, confirmed that the promotion was in the works but would happen only once he had settled into his role and found my replacement.

Weeks turned into months, and my promotion remained nothing more than a distant promise. One day, I mustered the courage to call Puneet about the progress. That's when I learned that the role I was being considered for had been made redundant due to restructuring. It was a relief to know I hadn't missed out on an opportunity, at least not yet, but the role was no longer available. If I had taken it, I might have found myself redundant too.

Dheeraj assured me that the promotion would take place the following year, but by then, the thrill of the initial announcement had worn off.

In the meantime, my team and I had our hands full with the growing complaints from cardholders about delayed or undelivered statements. Despite reorganizing the dispatch cycles and improving the process, the issue persisted. No matter how efficient we became, the problem seemed beyond our control.

As I reflected on the delay in my promotion, I couldn't help but wonder: Was it the promotion I had truly wanted, or was it the recognition and responsibility that I was after? And in that moment, I realized that sometimes, the journey itself provides more growth than the destination ever could.

Trails of a Different Kind

It all began in the heart of chaos, with two million cardholders and their ever-growing pile of grievances. The crux of their complaints? Statements—delayed, lost, or never delivered. It was a customer service nightmare, made worse by the fact that we relied on the Indian postal service, a system as old as the country's constitution but far less reliable.

We had done everything by the book—or so we thought. Statements were generated like clockwork and handed over to the post office within three days. With 15 statement cycles meticulously rejigged to balance the load, we even optimized for weekends. Yet, complaints rolled in like monsoon clouds.

As the manager in charge, I knew this wouldn't be solved by the usual boardroom brainstorming or motivational speeches. We needed to dig deeper, quite literally, into the postal sacks and the labyrinthine world of mail logistics.

It started with an idea born out of sheer desperation. My team and I seeded "dummy" statements—essentially fake mail addressed to team members across India. It was postal espionage, corporate-style. We tracked delivery times and delved into the operational black hole that was the General Post Office (GPO).

The findings? Fascinating, to say the least. At the GPO, mail was bundled into sacks and dispatched to airports. From there, the sacks flew to major locations daily. All seemed smooth, until we observed the chaos on the ground.

On Mondays or after holidays, the sheer volume of mail overwhelmed the system. The airport's mail vans, woefully undersized for the job, operated on a simple principle: last in, first out. As a result, some sacks spent days at the bottom of the heap. The problem cascaded at local post offices, where overburdened postmen played an unintentional game of "mail roulette."

Adding to the mess, statements sent to office addresses often reached desks only to find the recipient missing. It wasn't the fault of the postal service, nor entirely ours. It was a systemic flaw; one we couldn't fix. But we could pinpoint the root cause.

The Hunt for a Solution

Faced with a dilemma, we explored alternatives. But the cost of established couriers was far too high. Just as we thought we had hit a wall, a chance encounter during a trip to Delhi changed everything.

While still hunting for solutions, I took a break to visit my parents in Delhi. One evening, I noticed something peculiar: most of their letters arrived courtesy of a courier service I'd never heard of—BSA City Courier. Intrigued, I asked around and discovered that this mysterious service was also delivering mail to my in-laws.

Curiosity turned into action. I dialed the number printed on one of their envelopes and, within an hour, received a call from a man named Devesh Sachdev. His enthusiasm was palpable, and he offered to show me their operations. As luck would have it, he lived near my in-laws, making it easy to schedule a visit.

The next morning, Devesh picked me up and took me to BSA City Courier's office in Okhla. What I saw there was a revelation. Their model was simple yet effective: local deliveries at just ₹5, complete with proof of delivery and a 72-hour turnaround. It was the kind of efficiency the postal service could only dream of.

Back at the office, I shared the idea with Dheeraj. We both saw potential but also anticipated resistance. HSBC's vendor approval process was rigid, and true to form, the proposal was promptly rejected. The feedback? It was "neither advisable nor tenable."

But I wasn't ready to give up. As the business owner, we had the authority to push for exceptional approval. With no small amount of persuasion, we managed to greenlight a 90-day pilot project, limited to New Delhi.

Instead of handing over all statements to the post office, we segregated those bound for Delhi and sent them to BSA via Blue Dart. It was a gamble, but one worth taking.

Within three months, the results were unmistakable. Complaints about undelivered statements from New Delhi plummeted. Encouraged by this success, we requested BSA to expand its footprint gradually, rolling out their services across India.

What started as a small pilot soon expanded nationwide, transforming the way we managed statement deliveries. Devesh, once a stranger, had become a key partner and a close friend. Today, he is the CMD of a leading microfinance company. A testament to what vision and perseverance can achieve.

This episode taught me two invaluable lessons. First, no system is beyond improvement, but solutions often lie outside the usual playbook. It's the unconventional paths, like chasing down obscure courier services, that lead to breakthroughs. Second, relationships built during problem-solving can blossom into lifelong friendships.

But here's what I still ponder: How often do we overlook simple, local solutions because we're too focused on complex, global ones? Sometimes, the key to solving big problems lies in embracing small, overlooked opportunities. What's your "BSA moment" waiting to be discovered?

The Case of the Familiar Stranger

In my decades-long career in banking, I've handled my fair share of fires—some predictable, some bizarre, and others outright laughable. This was one of those episodes that tested my composure while nudging me to the edge of disbelief.

It began with an urgent call from our Head of Compliance. Her tone was terse, her words precise: "We have a situation. Someone has been withdrawing money from a high-profile customer's account. We suspect it's fraud."

The "high-profile customer" turned out to be none other than a senior functionary (DGM). When the apex regulator is involved, you tread carefully. Very carefully.

I reached out to the customer immediately. He was understandably livid. "How can your bank allow unauthorized transactions? The card has never left my wallet, and no one else knows the PIN!" His indignation was palpable, but so was his insistence that the bank was to blame. Two withdrawals, two weeks apart, had left his account lighter by a significant sum.

My instinct told me there was more to this story. I requested access to the ATM camera footage from our vendor. Two hours later, the recordings landed in my inbox.

The first frame froze my breath. Instead of the masked fraudster we all imagined, the footage revealed a young woman. Casual attire, hair tied back, and an air of nonchalance as she completed the transactions. On both occasions, it was the same girl.

Curiosity piqued; I arranged a meeting with the DGM at our office. To ensure diplomacy (and evidence), I requested Suren, with a knack for handling delicate situations, to join me in the meeting. As the customer settled into the conference room chair, I slid the laptop across the table and hit play.

The recording played in silence. Suren and I were watching him closely, not the screen. If there's one thing I've learned, it's that body language never lies. His reaction was...interesting. His face displayed a mix of emotions: confusion, shock, and something I couldn't quite place. Was it recognition? Embarrassment?

We didn't ask him anything. Just kept quiet.

"I can't say I know her," he muttered, his gaze lingering on the paused image of the girl withdrawing cash.

"Sir, this is concerning," I said, keeping my tone measured. "The PIN was used, and the card has been in your possession. Only someone who knows both could access the account."

Suren chimed in with his characteristic politeness. "We understand your frustration, sir. However, as per protocol, you'll need to file a police complaint. The bank will provide full support during the investigation."

The DGM nodded, but something in his demeanor shifted. He seemed...defensive. "Let me think this over," he said curtly before leaving.

By the time he reached the elevator, I had a gut feeling about how this story would end. And sure enough, the very next morning, we received an email from the customer.

"I have decided to withdraw my complaint. No further action is required," it read.

No explanation. No clarification. Just a quiet retreat. Suren and I exchanged a knowing glance when we read the email.

"Do you think...?" he began. I cut him off with a chuckle. "Let's just say, sometimes IT HAPPENS. And sometimes, it happens closer to home than one might admit."

Incidents like these teach you more about human nature than any leadership seminar ever could. People, no matter their rank or stature, are driven by a cocktail of emotions—pride, fear, and the instinct to protect what matters most, even if that "protection" means staying silent. We'll never know. What we do know is this: Life, much like banking, is full of surprises.

As I reflect on this quirky chapter in my career, I'm reminded of a bigger question: What would you do when faced with a dilemma that forces you to choose between the truth and your own pride?

WHIRLwind Adventures

HSBC, the global giant straddling 72 countries, was more than just a bank; it was an intricate ecosystem. One day, a directive arrived from the Group office's: our credit card business, a growing juggernaut, was to adopt a billion-dollar, plug-and-play technology platform. It was a state-of-the-art system, designed to process massive volumes and offer futuristic functionalities.

As the SPOC (Single Point of Contact) for the business side, I knew this wasn't just another project—it was going to be an odyssey. Our Malad office became the epicenter of this journey, which brought together over 100 people, two trial runs, countless sleepless nights, and one incredible finale.

The project kicked off with enthusiasm that soon collided with reality. The plug-and-play platform promised everything but required more customization than anticipated. Some features were irrelevant to our market. Conversely, crucial functionalities were glaringly absent.

Customization became our mantra. Dinaz, the project manager, led from the front, orchestrating the chaos with her trademark mix of diplomacy and discipline. From her corner office, she managed a battalion of project leads, each representing a function within the business. Dev, our IT Head, ensured technical feasibility, while the Group office in Hong Kong kept an eagle eye on progress.

As the months rolled by, our first trial run loomed large. The stakes were enormous, and the preparations intense. Scripts were created, scenarios were tested, and error logs became our new best friends. When the trial finally began, it was like watching a movie where the hero faces every possible obstacle before emerging victorious.

Error logs were meticulously prepared, tracked, and rectified. "This isn't a sprint, it's a marathon," Dinaz reminded us as we wrestled with bugs that seemed to multiply like rabbits. The team rallied together, fixing glitches with a mix of ingenuity and persistence.

Our Malad office had by now transformed into a war zone. Weekly meetings in the conference room were a cacophony of updates, questions, and the occasional heated debate. Dinaz ensured the chaos was contained, keeping presentations crisp and timelines sacred.

Meanwhile, monthly presentations to the Deputy CEO became high-stakes performances. Everyone rehearsed their slides as if auditioning for a movie. The pressure was palpable, but so was the camaraderie. We laughed at each other's jokes, shared late-night snacks, and celebrated small wins as a team.

The second trial run was the ultimate test of our efforts. By this time, the error logs had dwindled, and the system was showing promise. Spearheading this critical phase was Terrence, a sharp and unflappable IT expert from Hong Kong.

Terrence was a master of communication. He had a way of breaking down complex technical concepts into clear, actionable steps. His calm confidence became the anchor for the entire team. For 36 grueling hours, we worked together, testing every aspect of the system. The final activity was followed by a batch run—a rigorous simulation of real-world transactions.

When the last batch ran successfully, the room erupted in applause. Terrence smiled, nodded, and simply said, "Well done, team." It was the understated acknowledgment of a job well done, and it meant the world to all of us.

With the trials behind us, it was time to train the end-users. Workshops were held in the Malad office, webinars connected us to remote teams, and even late-night crash courses were conducted for the particularly stubborn participants.

D-Day: A Roaring Success

Launch day dawned with a mix of excitement and trepidation. The atmosphere in Malad was electric. Teams huddled around monitors, tracking every transaction processed by the new system. Terrence orchestrated the event like a seasoned conductor, ensuring every detail was monitored.

The final cutover activity began under Terrence's watchful eye. Clear, confident, and crisp, he led the team through the process with precision. When the system finally went live, it was as if the entire office held its breath.

And then it happened—the transactions began flowing smoothly. Every successful ping was greeted with cheers, and even the smallest glitches were addressed with lightning speed. By the end of the week, the system was stable, and the business was running like clockwork.

Looking back, this project was more than just an IT upgrade. It was a masterclass in resilience, collaboration, and the art of managing chaos. From the late-night calls to the heated debates, and from the glitches to the triumphs, every moment added to the tapestry of our success.

But amidst all the technology and tension, the human stories stood out: the shared laughter, the late-night pizza runs, and the camaraderie that made the impossible seem possible.

And yet, this experience left me with one lingering question:

In our relentless pursuit of progress, do we sometimes forget to celebrate the human connections that truly define our success?

CHAPTER 8

Encounters of a Different Kind

A Call to Action

The phone rang. It was Cheryl. "Dheeraj wants to meet you." For a moment, I felt like I'd been summoned to the principal's office. Unfortunately, my schedule resembled a Tetris game with no pause button. By the time I found myself free to meet him, Dheeraj had left for MG Road - Our Head Office. "He'll call," Cheryl reassured me.

And he did call. "Anil, I need to talk," he insisted, but his calendar was always chockablock. Eventually, the request faded into the background noise of daily operations. I convinced myself that it was probably about my promotion, long stuck in a bureaucratic vortex. Why stress over it? Promotions in corporate life, I reasoned, are like mangoes in monsoon—you wait, hope, and eventually get your hands sticky.

Days passed, and then one afternoon, Dheeraj summoned me with a surprising sense of urgency. "Come right away to my cabin." Something in his tone nudged me out of my comfortable procrastination.

When I arrived, he handed me a stack of email printouts, the corporate equivalent of a landmine. "Read these," he said, before adding casually, "Discuss with Anjan; he's been working on it."

I found Anjan, expecting clarity. Instead, I got a shrug that could have powered a wind turbine. "I don't know," he admitted. "I'm not able to figure a way out." Great. The metaphorical ball was now in my court, a heavy, spiked, flaming ball.

"Dheeraj," I reported back, "Anjan has shown his inability to assist."

Unfazed, he instructed, "There's a meeting with the Deputy CEO at 5 p.m. Please attend and keep me updated."

I grabbed a cab and sped toward MG Road, rehearsing mental somersaults for a meeting I barely understood. The DCEO's secretary ushered me in. The man himself, Nilesh Heredia, wasted no time.

"So, you're the guy," he declared, sizing me up like a cricket selector. He picked up his phone and summoned the Heads of the Compliance, Legal and HR departments. "Ensure he is given whatever support he needs - no questions will be asked. Just provide," he informed them.

When he asked for my plan, I played the only card I had. "I was informed about this today. Give me two days to analyze, understand the impact, and propose an action plan."

"Two days," he agreed. "Granted."

Back at the office, I sought data from HR and IT and plunged into it with the enthusiasm of a detective unraveling a noir mystery. The issue boiled down to the Hong Kong Monetary Authority's compliance guidelines on staff loans relative to annual compensation. 900+ staff were breaching the threshold. The glaring question loomed: What do we do?

I categorized the data—product-wise, region-wise, employee category-wise. By the next day, I had my plan ready. Reporting directly to the DCEO gave me a strange mix of freedom and fear. "How long will you need?" he asked.

"Thirty days," I replied, with a confidence I didn't entirely feel.

"Alright, I'll give you one extra week," he said, then added, "Report directly to me. This is my mobile number."

As I dove deeper, I realized the crux of the problem wasn't credit cards or personal loans—they were manageable. The real headache lay in home loans. Many of these were taken before employees joined HSBC, making them as sticky as gum on a new shoe.

I needed outside help. An acquaintance from the mortgage industry introduced me to a Credit Underwriting Head at a private bank. My proposal? A quasi-portfolio takeover of staff loans. After some rigorous due diligence, they agreed. That was the easy part.

The hard part was convincing our staff to migrate their loans to another bank. These weren't just numbers on a spreadsheet; they were people, spread across the country, each with their unique anxieties and doubts. I spent hours explaining options over the phone, attempting to sound both authoritative and empathetic.

Then came the next hurdle: coordination. The new bank's sales unit showed the kind of enthusiasm one expects from a teenager asked to clean their room. Our staff wasn't thrilled either.

Eventually, I stationed myself at the private bank's premises with Simon from my team, turning their office into a war room. A representative was assigned to us, and before long, I was mistaken for the new Business Head. It wasn't far from the truth—I was running their operations better than they were.

After weeks of negotiation, cajoling, and problem-solving, we managed to regularize the loans of all but two sub-staff employees. The deadline was met. Compliance was restored. Jobs were saved. Yet, the entire operation went unnoticed by the wider office. No applause. No ticker tape parade. Just the quiet satisfaction of knowing we'd averted disaster.

Looking back, the episode was a masterclass in juggling crisis management with creativity. It taught me that leadership often means taking ownership of problems no one else wants to touch.

But here's the reflection: Why is it that some of the most impactful work happens in the shadows, unnoticed and unsung? What do you think—should quiet victories be celebrated more loudly, or is the satisfaction of solving a problem its own reward?

A Close Call at the Supreme Court

The humidity in Mumbai's air did nothing to soothe my nerves that day. Sameer, my colleague, burst into my cabin, papers clutched tightly in his hand. He wasn't one to panic, but his face told a story of urgency.

"Supreme Court," he said, barely catching his breath. "There's a case against us—an NGO is accusing foreign bank credit card issuers of usurious charges. The hearing is next week."

I sat up straighter, the weight of his words settling into my chest. As a retail asset specialist with eight years of experience, I was no stranger to pressure. But this was different. This wasn't about numbers, compliance, or sales assurance. This was about defending our practices on the grandest stage of them all.

"Dheeraj said to do whatever it takes," Sameer continued, referring to our boss. "I've already started preparing detailed responses to the claimant's questions."

"Good," I said, trying to mask my own anxiety. "Let's get moving. We need the best legal counsel money can buy."

Sameer was a meticulous worker, and it showed in the dossier he had compiled. The data, ironically, was ready thanks to the very activist customers who regularly challenged our charges. They had unwittingly sharpened our defenses through their relentless queries.

For my part, I reviewed every page, adding inputs and ensuring no stone was left unturned. By the time we flew to Delhi for our first meeting with a senior Supreme Court advocate, we felt prepared, but far from confident.

Meeting the advocate, the first 'legal eagle', was an intimidating experience. His office was adorned with accolades and photographs amidst a showcase full of legal reference books.

We presented our case. He listened carefully, nodding at times and occasionally interrupting to ask clarifying questions. His analysis was sharp, and his understanding of the legal nuances impressed us. But his reluctance to commit fully made me uneasy.

"You'll be fine," he said, his tone almost dismissive. "Just let the court process unfold."

As we left his chambers, I turned to Sameer. "I don't know, Sameer. He's good, but something feels off. Let's get a second opinion."

Sameer hesitated, then nodded. "Agreed. We can't leave anything to chance.

A few weeks before the hearing, we were in New Delhi seeking his advice. The early hours of dawn in Delhi were cool, the city's usual chaos still tucked under a blanket of slumber. Sameer and I stood outside the gates of a sprawling bungalow, its stoned walls glowing faintly in the soft morning light.

Inside, we were told, lived one of India's most renowned legal luminaries.

Sameer looked at his watch: 6:58 a.m. "Are we really doing this?" he asked, his breath visible in the crisp air.

"We don't have a choice," I replied, gripping the stack of documents in my hand. "This case isn't just about compliance or regulations. It's about survival—ours and the banks."

The gate creaked open, revealing a man in simple white kurta-pajamas. He nodded and gestured for us to follow him into the garden.

The garden was breathtaking, even in the dim morning light. A manicured lawn stretched before us, dotted with ancient trees and blooming flowers that seemed to defy the city's pollution. At the center of it all sat the luminary himself, cross-legged on a wicker chair, a steaming cup of tea in hand.

"Good morning," he said, his voice deep and calm, as if he had all the time in the world.

We approached hesitantly, still unsure if this was a stroke of brilliance or an act of desperation. As we sat on the chairs provided, the aroma of fresh jasmine mingled with the earthy scent of dew. The setting was idyllic, but my mind was anything but at peace.

He motioned for us to begin, and Sameer launched into our case. His voice was steady, his explanation precise, honed through sleepless nights of preparation. The advocate listened intently, his sharp eyes betraying no emotion.

When Sameer finished, the silence was almost deafening. The advocate leaned back, took a long sip of his tea, and finally spoke. "Your arguments are solid. He outlined his perspective, echoing much of what we had already heard from the first advocate. "The judiciary will see the technicalities, but you must appeal to their sense of balance—between consumer protection and business operations."

His words were measured, wise even, but there was a nagging sense of incompletion. As the sun began to rise, bathing the garden in a golden hue, I couldn't shake the feeling that we were still walking a tightrope.

"Do you think we'll succeed?" I asked, breaking protocol by voicing my doubts aloud.

He smiled faintly, setting his cup down. "All you can do is be prepared."

We left the garden with a mix of hope and unease, the scent of jasmine following us out.

The next day, we stood outside the Supreme Court, its towering marble columns casting long shadows over the courtyard. Inside, the atmosphere was charged, a stark contrast to the serene garden where we'd sought counsel.

Our case was listed as no 102. We were there at 10 am sharp. As per our local legal officer, he expected our number won't come for hearing before 11:30 a.m., and as the morning wore on, I couldn't help but glance at my watch every few minutes. Sameer was unusually quiet.

At 11:15, our advocate was still nowhere to be seen. My palms began to sweat as I scanned the room, willing him to appear. "Where is he?" I muttered, his voice barely audible.

"He'll be here," Sameer said, though I wasn't sure if he believed it himself.

At 11:20, just as our case was called, our advocate strode in, his black robes flowing behind him like a superhero cape. He nodded at us, his expression calm but focused, and stepped forward to address the court.

The courtroom was silent. The judge, after hearing the complainant's advocate, asked for the respondent's submission. There was a silence. I wasn't sure why. Suddenly, our advocate began his submission. His arguments were concise, his demeanor commanding. As he spoke, I noticed other lawyers representing other foreign banks had yet to arrive.

It wasn't until later that we learned the truth: the senior-most advocate, hired by another bank, was delayed in another courtroom. By protocol, he would have spoken first, setting the tone for the defense. But his absence gave our advocate the rare albeit unplanned opportunity to make his case without interruption.

The judge listened intently, then announced, "Stay granted."

Relief flooded my chest, and I could see the tension drain from Sameer's face. The battle wasn't over, but we had won a crucial reprieve.

That evening, as we sat in the airport lounge waiting for our flight back to Mumbai, I replayed the events in my mind. The serene garden meeting, the chaotic courtroom, the unexpected stroke of luck—it all felt surreal.

Sameer leaned back in his chair, finally allowing himself to relax. "We were prepared," I said, "but I can't help thinking... what if the senior advocate had arrived on time?"

He nodded, stirring his coffee absentmindedly. "Luck played its part today, no doubt about it. But we were ready when the opportunity came. Maybe that's the real lesson: luck favors the prepared."

Unanticipated Triumph: The Promotion I Almost Forgot

One evening, I got a call from Dheeraj. The man was a force of nature, and I could tell that this call would be no different.

He wasn't in the office that day, having gone to attend some meeting at the head office, but somehow, he was still managing to send me a jolt of energy through the phone. The conversation started innocuously enough. He asked me to open his cabin.

Cheryl opened the door, and as I stood there, listening to Dheeraj on the phone, the anticipation mounted. He asked me to open his drawer. There was a brown envelope. A simple, innocuous brown envelope. I pulled it out, feeling a strange mixture of curiosity and dread. Dheeraj, still on the phone, encouraged me to open it. "Go on, open it," he urged.

I unfolded the envelope and, much to my surprise, instead of an assignment or new task, there it was. My promotion letter. My promotion letter. The one that I had removed from my memory long ago, thinking that the day would never come. The letter sat there, staring up at me as if it had been waiting for this moment, too. There was no fanfare. Just a few neatly printed words confirming what I had almost forgotten to expect—my long-awaited promotion.

I remember feeling a bit dazed, unsure if I was reading this right. I didn't even know what to say. "Well?" Dheeraj's voice crackled through the phone, his tone one of genuine mischief. "Happy?"

I fumbled for words, still processing the shock. "Uh... It's fine. Thanks." The words tumbled out of my mouth, almost too awkwardly for the occasion. I had spent months trying to push the idea of promotion from my mind, seeing it as some distant event that would never happen, always buried under deadlines, reviews, and the mountains of work that filled my day. Yet here it was, a letter that I hadn't even dared to hope for.

Now, looking back, I realize the strange timing of it all. For months, I had been hoping for this overdue promotion but had somehow convinced myself it was just a pipe dream. It didn't help that Dheeraj had been relentlessly chasing the higher-ups on my behalf. His persistence was almost a constant echo in the office.

But here's the thing: even though Dheeraj had tirelessly followed up, there was an underlying truth I had to face. Some things simply aren't within your control. No matter how much you push, some processes take time. There are always external factors at play that you can't change, and that's something I had to learn the hard way. At that moment, when the letter was placed in my hands, I realized that all I had to do was focus on the job in front of me. Let the results follow. Keep doing my best. It's easy to forget that sometimes when you're in the trenches, pushing for your moment to shine.

Dheeraj's playful chuckle echoed in my ear as I hung up the phone. I stood there in his cabin for a moment, just looking at the letter, letting the weight of it sink in. The thing was, in all honesty, I hadn't needed the promotion to feel validated. But boy, did it feel good to know that someone—someone who had fought for me and championed my cause—had helped me get to that point.

Now, after all these years, as I reflect on that moment, I'm reminded of how many times we go through life trying to rush to the finish line. We push for promotions, titles, and recognition, sometimes forgetting that the journey is just as important as the destination.

So, here's my question to you, dear reader: How often do we find ourselves waiting for that promotion, that acknowledgment, that validation—only to realize that it was never really about the end goal? Perhaps, like me, we need to focus on doing our best, day in and day out, and let the results come as they may. It's not your failure but a setback, and one must overcome it with positivity.

It's Lonely and Slippery at the Top: Leadership in the Face of Crisis

Corporate leadership often feels like a tightrope walk, balancing ambitions with realities, growth with sustainability. But when that balance is disrupted by unforeseen developments, or worse, deliberate malintent, the fall can be hard and unforgiving. It was during one such period of reckoning that I witnessed the essence of leadership through the resolute actions of Dheeraj, our Business Head of Retail Assets. His ethos, resilience, and ability to lead through the storm left an indelible mark on me.

When the Curtain Fell

The retail assets division had been a cornerstone of our Personal Banking for years. It was a story of growth, innovation, and meticulous effort by hundreds of dedicated individuals. But even the strongest structures can collapse if termites work unseen within the walls. A series of systemic flaws that had gone unnoticed—revealed the fragile foundation upon which the division rested.

The discovery was devastating. Years of hard work were compromised, and trust, both internal and external, was shaken. The business had become unsustainable, and after much deliberation, the inevitable decision was made: the division would be shut down, and the organization would undergo restructuring.

It was a decision that sent ripples of uncertainty and fear through the company. For Dheeraj, the head of the division, it was more than just a professional setback; it was personal. He had built the business line, nurtured it like a child, and now he had to dismantle it with his own hands.

Dheeraj's leadership style was rooted in clarity, integrity, and empathy—qualities that shone even brighter in the face of adversity. While the rest of us grappled with the enormity of the situation, Dheeraj remained a pillar of composure. "Leadership isn't about avoiding crises," he often said. "It's about standing tall when they come."

But even pillars can feel the weight of the world. At home, Dheeraj was mourning the loss of his father-in-law, a man he deeply respected. On the day of the funeral, I saw him perform the last rites with tear-streaked cheeks, his grief laid bare. Yet, that same evening, he stood before the India CEO, delivering a presentation on the crisis, the collapse of retail assets, and the way forward.

He didn't hide the bitter truths. He spoke candidly about the systemic issues, and the tough decisions that lay ahead. His ability to confront the situation head-on, while shouldering personal loss, was nothing short of remarkable.

With the decision to wind down retail assets, the next step was implementing a massive restructuring. Over 700 employees across various functions were affected, and Dheeraj insisted on leading the charge himself.

"This is our family," he told me when I hesitated about being part of the restructuring team. "As elders, it's our responsibility to see them through this—not just with decisions, but with dignity."

Townhall meetings became our platform to communicate with employees. Dheeraj believed in transparency, even when the truth was difficult to hear.

"We're here because a few lost sight of the values that this company stands for," he said during the first meeting. "But as a family, we must bear this burden together. These decisions are not a reflection of your abilities, but of the circumstances we find ourselves in."

The room was silent, but the weight of his words hung heavy in the air.

My Tryst with Restructuring

Abhijit

As a member of the management team, I was also tasked with the difficult job of handling redundancy interviews. One interview stands out vividly in my memory, even though it was 16 years ago.

A young junior executive, Abhijit, with just three years of experience, walked in. He was confident, but as soon as I broke the news of his redundancy, his demeanor changed. He was shocked, and to my surprise, he began to sob. He had been told by his manager that he had to appear for an interview for a new role. Abhi was carrying his CV and his last three years' performance appraisals were all 'outstanding'.

Abhi's story was heart-wrenching. He explained his family's financial struggles, his father was retired and had heart bypass surgery, for which he had taken a loan, and how he had studied under street lights to become the sole breadwinner. He refused to leave the room.

The HR partner, alongside me, was equally clueless. I was taken aback and didn't know how to react. Something about Abhi's simplicity, his past performance, and the sheer misfortune of being ill-advised tugged at my heart. I assured him of my help. In a personal capacity, I offered to pay his current salary for the next three months to support him.

That night, I couldn't shake off the image of Abhi's tearful face. The next day, fate intervened. Sanjay, a friend who worked at another bank, called me. I shared Abhi's story, and Sanjay mentioned he had a vacancy he hadn't planned to fill. Intrigued by Abhi's determination, Sanjay agreed to meet him.

I called Abhi, urging him to meet Sanjay. The meeting was a success. Abhi was selected and started his new role soon. Abhi's journey at the new bank wasn't smooth sailing. Initially, there was resistance from some senior staff who doubted his abilities. However, Sanjay saw something special in Abhi and decided to mentor him personally. Abhi's dedication, combined with Sanjay's guidance, helped him quickly adapt and excel in his role. Abhi worked tirelessly, continuously improving his skills. He even pursued an executive MBA. Each step was a testament to his resilience and determination.

And today, from a young man on the verge of losing everything, is a triumphant Vice President in a leading Indian bank.

Was it destiny? Hard work? A bit of both?

Abhijit's story taught me invaluable leadership lessons. It reminded me of the importance of empathy, the impact of mentoring, and the power of resilience. Sometimes, offering support can change someone's life, and sometimes, believing in someone's potential can lead to extraordinary outcomes.

Debendu

In the high-stakes world of sales, where performance is the ultimate currency, Debendu was a star—until life threw him off guard. He was one of our most energetic and passionate sales officers, consistently delivering results. But personal issues forced him to take a long break to recuperate and rehabilitate.

When he returned, eager to reestablish his rhythm, I decided to bring him into our Sales Assurance team as a trainer. This team was composed of the best performers, and he quickly began to catch up. However, during annual appraisals, his rating suffered under the rigid bell curve methodology, despite no adverse marks on his performance.

Life took another unexpected turn on account of the restructuring, which had impacted all functions. We scrambled to minimize the fallout by showcasing our team members to other divisions. Our team's reputation meant most were quickly absorbed, but his last rating held him back. I was deeply concerned for him. He had just recovered from a significant personal challenge, and now faced professional uncertainty.

I sat down with him, encouraging him to stay positive and keep all options open, including relocation if necessary. I also reached out to his father and wife, urging them to provide unwavering emotional support. Our team rallied around him, assisting him in exploring internal vacancies and preparing for interviews. Despite our collective efforts, by the deadline, he still had no offers.

I noticed a suitable role in the South, managed by someone who had previously been part of our division. When I called to inquire, the manager praised Debendu's capabilities but hesitated due to his last rating. I asked him a simple yet profound question: "If you were in Debendu's position, how would you feel?" I urged him to give him a six-month time to prove himself. If he didn't meet expectations, he could be let go.

The manager agreed, and Debendu got the chance he desperately needed. Six months later, Debendu not only met but exceeded expectations. His resilience, coupled with the unwavering support from his family and our team, allowed him to turn his situation around.

This experience taught me valuable lessons about leadership and team management. Understanding and addressing the emotional and personal challenges of team members is crucial. Building a strong support system, encouraging family involvement and peer support can make a world of difference for someone facing tough times.

Giving second chances can lead to remarkable transformations, and proactively tracking and supporting team members' progress ensures they receive the necessary guidance and opportunities. Debendu's journey reinforced my belief that true leadership is about fostering growth, resilience, and trust. It's about creating an environment where every individual can thrive, even when the odds are against them.

The days that followed were grueling. Every conversation, every decision, was fraught with emotion. Employees came to us seeking answers, reassurance, or just someone to vent to.

One senior employee, with tears in his eyes, asked Dheeraj, "How do you make these decisions and still sleep at night?" Dheeraj's response was measured but heartfelt. "You don't," he admitted. "Leadership is lonely. It means making decisions that no one else wants to, knowing that you'll never be universally liked or understood. But it also means carrying the weight of those decisions so that others don't have to."

His words stayed with me. For Dheeraj, leadership wasn't about power or recognition, it was about responsibility.

Amidst the restructuring, we also saw the less savory side of corporate life. As the situation unfolded, whispers of blame and backroom politics began to emerge. Some saw the crisis as an opportunity to settle old scores or curry favor with leadership. Others sought to distance themselves, hoping to escape the fallout unscathed.

Dheeraj, however, refused to engage in the mudslinging. "Corporate politics can only distract you if you let it," he told me one evening. "Focus on what's right, and let the rest fall away."

This wasn't just talk. Dheeraj consistently led by example, keeping his focus on the employees, the restructuring process, and the future of the organization. His integrity became a guiding light for the rest of us, even when the environment around us grew increasingly toxic.

As the restructuring neared its conclusion, we held one last town hall meeting. The room was filled with those who remained, employees who had weathered the storm but carried the scars of what we had been through.

Dheeraj stood before them, his voice steady but tinged with emotion. "This has been one of the most challenging periods in our company's history," he began. "But it has also shown us the strength and resilience of this family. The road ahead won't be easy, but together, we will rebuild, stronger and better."

The applause that followed wasn't thunderous; it was subdued, reflective. It wasn't just an acknowledgment of his words, but of his leadership.

Looking back, I realized that this crisis was about the rise of true leadership, not the fall of a business line. Dheeraj's ability to face adversity with honesty, empathy, and resolve was a masterclass in what it means to lead.

He taught me that leadership isn't about avoiding tough decisions, but standing firm in the face of them. It's about carrying the burden of responsibility, even when it feels crushing. And above all, it's about staying true to your values, no matter how chaotic the world around you becomes.

As I reflect on those turbulent months, I'm left with a question: When leadership becomes lonely and the weight of the world rests on your shoulders, will you stand tall—or will you falter?

In the bustling corridors of HSBC, where each desk buzzed with ambition and urgency, my career took an unexpected yet intriguing turn. Dheeraj, my colleague and a friend, had just transitioned to head the SME banking division after our exhaustive stint in a demanding exercise. I, too, soon found myself stepping into uncharted territory, albeit in a completely different domain. The opportunity to lead the Relationship Management team within the Technology Division's Change Management function appeared like a fork in my career's path. Little did I know, this role would redefine my perception of leadership, challenge, and personal growth.

Turning the Wheels of Change

Change Management wasn't merely about technology; it was about connecting the dots between complex business operations and seamless technological solutions. At the heart of this function was a seven-member team of Relationship Managers, each responsible for a critical business line. Corporate, Commercial, Retail, Treasury, Custodial Services, and Cash Management – each domain came with its unique quirks and challenges. My role was to provide clarity, direction, and synergy among these diverse elements.

Coming from years of experience in the banking sector, I knew the language of business like the back of my hand. But this role demanded more – a deep understanding of technology, an empathetic ear for operational issues, and the ability to translate technical solutions into tangible benefits for the business heads.

I dove in headfirst, using every ounce of my leadership experience to cultivate trust and collaboration within my team. Early on, I realized that each Relationship Manager faced an uphill battle – convincing business stakeholders of the value of technological change was no easy task. My job was to ensure my team felt supported, valued, and equipped to overcome resistance.

Slowly but surely, we began to make a mark. The team's proactive approach won hearts and minds. Instead of waiting for crises, we anticipated needs, creating solutions that aligned with business goals. Treasury appreciated the seamless integration of new risk-management tools. Retail banking lauded the simplification of customer onboarding processes and Corporate banking benefited from streamlined reporting systems that allowed quicker decision-making.

Each success story wasn't just a feather in our cap but a testament to the potential of collaboration. Over time, our efforts were recognized beyond the walls of our office. At the annual regional awards ceremony, our team was named "Best in Asia" – a proud moment that underscored how far we had come.

Yet, despite the accolades, a curious restlessness began to creep in. Unlike my earlier roles, where every day was a battle to meet targets or navigate unpredictable markets, this role felt... peaceful. The challenges seemed more procedural than existential. With the systems in place and the team excelling, there was little left to prove.

Success, ironically, became a source of monotony. I started to question my own motivation. What was next? Could I sustain the same level of energy and passion in a role where the excitement of overcoming adversity was replaced by predictable rhythms?

It was during this phase of introspection that life tested me in an uncharted territory – one that forced me to reassess not just my career but my priorities.

CHAPTER 9

The Twilight of a 30-year Legacy at HSBC: Lessons, Legacy, and Closure

Back home in New Delhi, a property dispute that had simmered beneath the surface for years erupted into a full-blown crisis. The legalities were draining, not just financially but emotionally. Resolving it required my undivided attention, and balancing this personal exigency with the demands of work became increasingly untenable.

In 1984, when I first joined HSBC, I was stepping into a world I didn't fully understand but was eager to embrace. By the time I left in April 2012, I had navigated nearly three decades of immense learning, growth, and evolution—both personally and professionally. Those years shaped my perspective, honed my skills, and left me with lessons that would guide me for the rest of my life.

Learning Through Observation

From day one, I was aware of the importance of observing those around me. My managers, peers, and even my team members became my greatest teachers.

Some managers left a lasting impression, teaching me what leadership truly means. They led with integrity, clarity, and purpose. One of my first managers emphasized the importance of precision and discipline. "Banking is about trust," he would say, “and trust comes from doing the small things right.” This advice stayed with me throughout my career.

Another manager taught me the power of delegation and empowerment. He trusted me with responsibilities that seemed daunting at first, but his confidence in my abilities inspired me to deliver. That experience showed me how leaders could unlock potential in their teams by giving them room to grow.

But not all lessons came from positive examples. Some managers, through their shortcomings, taught me what not to do. I worked under a leader who managed through fear and micromanagement. The atmosphere he created was stifling, and it affected the morale and performance of the team. From him, I learned that respect and trust are far more effective motivators than fear.

Another manager avoided making decisions, often leaving the team in a state of confusion. That experience reinforced the importance of decisiveness in leadership. A leader’s role, I realized, is to provide direction, even if the path isn’t entirely clear. Indecision can be more damaging than a wrong decision.

Mastering All Facets of Banking

Over the years, I was fortunate to work across various aspects of banking. From Personal banking and institutional banking to trade finance, operations, and customer service, each role added a new layer to my understanding of the industry.

Retail banking taught me the importance of customer relationships. I learned that every customer interaction was an opportunity to build trust and loyalty. Listening to their needs and finding solutions that worked for them became second nature.

In Trade services and Institutional banking, I discovered the art of negotiation and relationship management. The stakes were higher, the decisions more complex, but the principles remained the same—focus on long-term value rather than short-term gain while keeping a hawk eye on compliance and regulatory mandates.

Operations management was where I truly appreciated the balance between efficient processes and controls. It was about understanding the bigger picture, analyzing data and trends, reviewing inefficiencies and making informed decisions.

Through these diverse experiences, I gained a holistic understanding of banking. More importantly, I developed a deep appreciation for teamwork. No aspect of banking operates in isolation. Success in one area depends on collaboration across functions.

Leadership and Mentorship

As I climbed the ranks, I transitioned from being an executor to a leader. My focus shifted from delivering results to enabling others to succeed.

One of the most rewarding aspects of my career was mentoring young professionals. I took pride in guiding them, sharing my experiences, and helping them navigate their own challenges. Some of them went on to achieve great success, and knowing I played a small part in their journey was immensely fulfilling.

Leadership also came with its share of challenges. I learned that no decision would ever satisfy everyone, but what mattered was the intent behind the decision and how it was communicated. Transparency and empathy became cornerstones of my leadership style.

The Lessons I Carried

As I reflect on those years, a few key lessons stand out:

1. Integrity is Non-Negotiable

In banking, integrity isn't just a value, it's the foundation of the profession. Every decision, no matter how small, must be made with honesty and fairness.

2. People are at the Heart of Everything

Whether it was customers, colleagues, or teams, the human aspect of banking was always central. Understanding and respecting people's needs, perspectives, and contributions made all the difference.

3. Adaptability is a Superpower

Over nearly three decades, the industry transformed—from manual processes to digital innovation, from local operations to global integration. The ability to adapt, learn, and evolve was crucial to staying relevant.

4. Leadership is About Trust, Not Control

Micromanagement stifles growth, while trust empowers teams. As a leader, my role was to guide, support, and enable, not dictate.

5. Failures are the Best Teachers

Not every decision I made was perfect. But every misstep taught me something valuable. Failure isn't the end—it's part of the journey.

6. Failures and Setbacks are Not the Same

Setbacks are temporary obstacles; failures are outcomes that didn't go as planned. Both offer valuable lessons. Growth comes when we stop fearing them and start learning from them.

The Day I Walked Away

On my last day at HSBC, I spent time reflecting. I walked through the office, thinking about the milestones, the challenges, and the people who had shaped my journey. There was a sense of closure but also a deep sense of gratitude.

As I handed over my responsibilities, I felt a mix of emotions. There was pride in what I had accomplished, but also a tinge of sadness at leaving behind something that had been such an integral part of my life.

I didn't leave with a physical legacy; there were no plaques or awards. My legacy, I believed, was in the people I had worked with, the teams I had built, and the values I had upheld.

Walking out of the building for the last time was bittersweet. But I knew it was time to move on. HSBC had given me more than a career; it had given me purpose, perspective, and a lifetime of lessons.

As I moved into the next chapter of my life, I carried those lessons with me. They became the foundation of my approach to coaching and leadership, reminding me that every ending is also a new beginning.

Looking back, my time at HSBC wasn't just a job or a career—it was a journey of growth, relationships, and transformation. And while that chapter has closed, the lessons it taught me continue to guide me every day.

03

REBIRTH IN A NEW DAWN

CHAPTER 10

Beneath African Skies: Where Restless Roots Meet New Horizons

It was an unremarkable evening when the call came, but little did I know it would change the trajectory of my life. I was at home when my phone buzzed. The caller ID displayed a familiar name: Dheeraj.

Years earlier, Dheeraj and I had worked together at HSBC. He was someone I admired for his strategic brilliance and bold leadership. Since then, he had taken up the role of Group Managing Director and Chief Executive Officer of a distinguished African banking institution. His call that evening wasn't just a friendly check-in, it carried the kind of opportunity that comes wrapped in both challenge and intrigue.

"Anil, I've heard about your departure from HSBC," he began. His tone was direct but warm, characteristic of the man I knew. "How open are you to relocating to Malawi?"

The question hung in the air for a moment.

Malawi?

The name barely registered. My mind raced, trying to place this unfamiliar country on the map. Was it near Kenya? South Africa? Or was it one of those smaller nations tucked away in the vast tapestry of the African continent? I realized I didn't have the faintest idea.

"Malawi," I repeated slowly, more to myself than to Dheeraj. "Honestly, I'm not entirely sure where it is. But if it means working with you again, I'm open to it."

Dheeraj chuckled. "I'll take that as a yes," he said. "Let me work out some details, and I'll get back to you."

The call ended, but the seed of curiosity had been planted. Later that night, I found myself diving into a crash course on Malawi. Known as the "Warm Heart of Africa," it was a landlocked country brimming with natural beauty, from the vast expanse of Lake Malawi to its rolling hills and welcoming people. As enchanting as it sounded, I wasn't entirely convinced that uprooting my life for an unknown land was the right move.

A week later, Dheeraj called again. This time, he had a different proposition.

"Anil, there's been a change. A new position has opened up in Botswana. The bank needs someone to manage its operations there. I thought of you immediately."

Botswana. Now, this name stirred a different kind of curiosity. I had heard of it, primarily as a land of diamonds and deserts, with a reputation for political stability and economic growth. As Dheeraj spoke, outlining the role and its challenges, I felt the familiar spark of excitement that comes with the prospect of charting new territories.

"Let's do it," I said, my decision made.

Botswana: A Jewel in the Heart of Southern Africa

Nestled in the southern part of Africa, Botswana is a landlocked country renowned for its stunning natural landscapes, vibrant culture, and exemplary governance. From its historical roots to its contemporary development, Botswana is a country that often stands apart from the rest of Africa in significant ways. My stint allowed me to delve deeper into this remarkable nation, uncovering its unique traits, rich history, and steadfast values.

Botswana's story begins with its indigenous peoples, the San (Bushmen), who are among the oldest inhabitants of Africa. Their rock paintings and oral traditions offer a glimpse into a time when the land was untamed and deeply connected to nature. The arrival of the Bantu-speaking Tswana people around 2000 years ago marked the next chapter in the nation's history. The Tswana tribes established a socio-political structure that emphasized consensus and unity, a characteristic still evident in Botswana's modern-day governance.

During the colonial period, Botswana, then known as Bechuanaland, came under British protection in 1885 to prevent encroachment by neighboring powers, particularly South Africa. However, unlike many African nations, Botswana retained significant autonomy during its colonial era, as the British exercised minimal interference in its internal affairs. This allowed Botswana to preserve its traditional institutions and social cohesion, setting the stage for a smoother transition to independence.

In 1966, Botswana achieved independence with Seretse Khama as its first president. A visionary leader, Khama steered the country toward democracy and sustainable development. Unlike many post-colonial African nations that grappled with authoritarianism and instability, Botswana emerged as a beacon of political stability.

Its political system is founded on the principles of accountability, transparency, and respect for the rule of law. Elections are held regularly, and power transitions have been peaceful, earning Botswana a reputation as one of the least corrupt countries in Africa.

The discovery of diamonds shortly after independence could have led to the "resource curse" seen in other African nations. However, Botswana leveraged its diamond wealth to invest in education, healthcare, and infrastructure, lifting its people out of poverty and building a robust economy. Its prudent management of resources is a lesson in foresight and integrity.

Botswana is considered one of the safest countries in Africa. During my stay in Gaborone, I noticed how secure and orderly the city felt, even at night. The government's emphasis on law enforcement, combined with a generally peaceful population, has contributed to low crime rates.

Unlike many African nations facing insurgencies, ethnic conflicts, or terrorism, Botswana has managed to avoid these issues. Its homogeneity—nearly 80% of the population belongs to the Tswana ethnic group—has played a role in maintaining national unity. However, the government also actively promotes inclusivity and discourages ethnic division, fostering a strong sense of community.

Botswana's geography is dominated by the Kalahari Desert, which covers about 70% of its landmass. However, the country's true natural gem is the Okavango Delta, a UNESCO World Heritage Site and one of the world's largest inland deltas. During my exploration of Botswana, I was struck by the sheer contrast between the arid desert landscapes and the lush, water-filled expanses of the delta.

This geographical diversity contributes to Botswana's incredible biodiversity. The delta and surrounding areas are home to a dazzling array of wildlife, including elephants, lions, leopards, and endangered African wild dogs. Botswana's commitment to conservation is unparalleled; almost 40% of its land is dedicated to national parks and wildlife reserves, making it a top destination for eco-tourism.

Botswana's national parks are among its greatest treasures. Chobe National Park, home to the largest population of elephants in Africa, offers some of the continent's most breathtaking wildlife encounters. Moremi Game Reserve in the Okavango Delta is a haven for birdwatchers and safari enthusiasts.

What sets Botswana apart is its low-impact tourism model. Unlike other countries that prioritize mass tourism, Botswana focuses on high-value, low-volume tourism to minimize environmental degradation. This approach ensures that its national parks remain pristine and uncrowded, providing visitors with an intimate connection to nature.

Gaborone: A Modern African Capital

Gaborone, the capital city, is a fascinating blend of tradition and modernity. My stay in a suburban hotel revealed the city's quiet charm, far removed from the hustle and bustle typical of many African capitals. Gaborone is not a city of towering skyscrapers or flashy opulence; instead, it is a well-organized, laid-back metropolis that prioritizes functionality and sustainability.

One of the most striking aspects of Botswana is the dignity of labor. From hotel staff to street vendors, everyone takes pride in their work. There is a palpable sense of equality and mutual respect in how people interact. It was inspiring to see how service industry workers carried out their duties with professionalism and a sense of purpose, regardless of the task.

The streets of Gaborone are clean and well-maintained, reflecting the city's commitment to orderliness. While it lacks the grandeur of larger cities, its unassuming character and warmth make it uniquely appealing.

Peculiar Yet Unique Traits

Botswana has several peculiar traits that make it stand out. For instance, its dual legal system incorporates both customary and common law, allowing traditional leaders to play a role in governance. This blending of old and new ensures that the country's heritage remains intact while it progresses into the modern era.

Another distinctive feature is the country's emphasis on consultation, known as "kgotla." This traditional forum allows citizens to voice their opinions and participate in decision-making, fostering a sense of ownership and accountability.

Dumela Rra

When I moved to Botswana for my banking stint, I expected a quiet, routine life in a small African country. Landing in Botswana as an Indian expat, I quickly realized I was in for an adventure unlike any other. Working in a bank, far from the hustle of Mumbai and the orderliness of Singapore, Botswana's charm lies in its delightful peculiarities, welcoming culture, and unique sense of humor that's as dry as the Kalahari itself.

What I discovered was a world filled with surprising cultural intricacies, warm friendships, and the unique resilience of a society that, in some ways, reminded me of the vibrant, ambitious atmosphere of Dubai—but with zebras instead of Lamborghinis.

Botswana's culture is deeply rooted in respect and gentleness. While Indians are known for our "rough talk" and directness, I quickly learned that in Botswana, it's all about politeness and quiet communication. The Tswana people are sensitive to tone and approach, something I found both refreshing and a bit challenging. You don't raise your voice in Botswana; you raise your empathy. A misplaced "what?!" can come across as an affront, while a gentle nod and a smile can open doors to new friendships.

The Land of Pula: Rain or Cash, It's All the Same Here

In Botswana, the word "pula" does double duty—it's both the currency and the word for rain. Now, as someone used to monsoon downpours, I found it amusing that in a country where rain is a rarity, it's literally worth its weight in gold (or diamonds, in Botswana's case). Imagine my confusion during my first week when someone greeted me with "Pula!" I thought they were trying to hand me a tip—turns out, they were just saying hello. Talk about a warm (and financially confusing) welcome!

Matriarchy and Strong Women: The Silent Backbone

Botswana's societal structure is intriguing, with a strong presence of matriarchal elements. Women in Botswana often play pivotal roles, both at home and in the community. Although not overtly matriarchal like some traditional societies, women in Botswana are highly respected and influential, quietly steering family decisions and community affairs.

This respect extends into cultural practices, such as lobola (bride price), a custom still widely practiced. Unlike the dowry system familiar to many Indians, lobola is seen as a gesture of respect and commitment rather than a financial burden. The groom's family gives cattle or cash to the bride's family, symbolizing the value of the woman being brought into the family—though with a modern twist, like negotiating the price based on one's education or professional achievements. It's like negotiating a contract with your in-laws; who said marriage isn't a business deal?

Capital Bank: A Journey of Leadership and Legacy

Nestled along the bustling Lobatse Road in Gaborone, Botswana, Capital Bank stood as a beacon of trust and stability. The two-story building, clean and well-maintained, reflected a sense of quiet professionalism. The ground floor housed the branch, where daily customer interactions unfolded, while the head office was situated at the rear. The first floor was dedicated to support functions, providing a sense of hierarchy and order within the space. Green, the signature color of Capital Bank, painted the walls, symbols of growth and harmony, fostering an environment that felt both secure and welcoming.

The bank was a trusted institution within Botswana's financial landscape, but beneath its polished exterior, challenges simmered. The senior management team was composed mostly of expatriates from India and Zimbabwe, creating a diverse but often disconnected environment. The local staff, primarily Setswana speakers, seemed reserved, skeptical, and unsure of the leadership brought in from abroad. It was in this environment that I landed as the Chief Operating Officer (COO).

Upon my appointment as COO, I was entrusted with managing almost all operational functions of the bank, except for credit, human resources (HR), and marketing. The task ahead of me was clear but daunting. I needed to align a team that had previously been under the direction of expatriates, many of whom had left a trail of inefficiencies and unresolved tensions. My mission was to bridge the gap between the expatriate managers and the local staff, fostering a sense of trust, ownership, and accountability.

When I first met my team of nine departmental managers, I could feel their wariness. They were skeptical, reserved, and, at times, apprehensive. They had seen expatriates come and go, each bringing their own set of policies, often leaving behind confusion or frustration. These were not easy shoes to fill. I knew that to succeed, I had to take a different approach—one that involved engaging with my team on a personal level.

Sholo: The Unlikely Teacher

In my first few weeks, I was fortunate to find an unexpected ally in Sholo, the tea lady. She was more than just the person who kept the office supplied with coffee and tea; she was a source of warmth and wisdom, always offering a smile or a kind word to anyone who needed it. Sholo quickly became my guide in learning Setswana, teaching me essential greetings and cultural nuances. Her enthusiasm was contagious, and I made a point of learning from her every day.

One afternoon, during a team meeting, I greeted everyone with the simple Setswana phrase, "Dumelang bagaetsho," meaning "Hello, my people." The room lit up immediately, and I could sense a shift in the dynamic. It was small, but it mattered. Sholo's patience and encouragement helped me break down cultural barriers, and in return, I became more connected with my team. The staff began to see me not as an outsider but as someone who was willing to understand their language, culture, and values.

Hit the Ground Running

As I settled into my role, I was given two immediate deliverables: foreign exchange reconciliation and a long-delayed software implementation for the finance department. Both were critical, and both were in disarray.

Forex reconciliation was a mess. There were discrepancies dating back several years. The Treasury team seemed overwhelmed, unable to pinpoint the source of the issues.

Meanwhile, the software implementation for the finance department was similarly plagued by delays and confusion. The vendor sent a representative once a week, but the software was so poorly suited for banking operations that it could never generate a balance sheet. I discovered that the software was intended for a manufacturing company, not a bank, which made it entirely unsuitable for our needs.

I was determined to address both of these challenges head-on, but I knew I needed to first earn the trust of the team before I could implement any significant changes under my area of responsibility.

I began by meeting with each departmental manager one-on-one, taking time to understand their concerns and ideas. They were skeptical of yet another expatriate leader, but I was committed to proving that I was different. I made it clear that I valued their insights and wanted to empower them to take ownership of their work.

I discovered that they didn't have any documented processes for their daily tasks. They knew their jobs well, but there was no formal structure or consistency. This was a critical gap, especially in a financial institution where precision and accountability are paramount. I decided that we needed to document every process, and I set aside time every day to meet with managers and their teams to map out each activity step-by-step.

With a whiteboard on the wall, we went through each process and jotted down the key steps. At the end of each session, I took a picture of the whiteboard and used it as a foundation for creating formal process documentation. These processes were later reviewed by me and the bank's auditor to ensure they met regulatory standards.

The team began to see the value of this exercise. The staff, once disengaged, started taking ownership of the new processes. As we reviewed the steps and refined them, we improved efficiencies and began eliminating bottlenecks. This was a turning point for both the staff and me—we had found a way to work together.

Taka: The Calm Problem-Solver

During this process, Taka, the IT Manager, quickly became one of my most trusted allies. Taka was calm under pressure, methodical, and always focused on finding solutions. Whether it was fixing a technical glitch or troubleshooting a system issue, Taka handled it with grace and precision. He was more than just a problem solver; he was a source of stability in an otherwise chaotic environment.

One particular instance stands out. A customer had filed a complaint about the service levels in the branch, claiming that he had waited for over 30 minutes without being attended to. This complaint was escalated to the CEO, and I was tasked with investigating it. Taka and I reviewed the camera footage from that day. To our surprise, the customer had been served within 15 minutes. It turned out that the complaint was fabricated by the customer, who was influenced by someone within the bank.

When I confronted the customer with the footage, he was visibly shaken and apologized for his actions. This was a turning point for me. Taka's expertise not only resolved the issue but also helped expose the underhanded tactics being employed by certain individuals in the bank. It was a victory for transparency and integrity.

A Tale of Transformation, Turmoil, and Growth

When I accepted the role of Chief Operating Officer at Capital Bank, headquartered in Malawi but with strong footprints across Southern Africa, I envisioned a challenging yet fulfilling journey. The mandate was clear: to make the bank's operations and technology robust and efficient, setting the foundation for sustainable high growth. Yet, beneath the surface of this ambitious agenda lay a complex web of relationships, power dynamics, and simmering tensions.

Capital Bank was no ordinary institution. Owned by a close-knit group of high net-worth businessmen of Indian origin from Kenya, Malawi, and Botswana, the bank operated with the drive of private enterprise but also carried the baggage of old-school banking practices. At the helm was CEO Gade, a seasoned ex-SBI senior manager, whose experience was matched by his entourage—two former SBI veterans overseeing credit and treasury. Their collective understanding of traditional banking was formidable, but it was also steeped in a reluctance to embrace modern practices.

I stepped in as COO with a fresh perspective and a transformative agenda. My role encompassed all functions except credit, treasury, HR, and marketing. Additionally, I was tasked with two critical projects: reconciling two years' worth of unresolved foreign exchange transactions and overseeing the migration of the bank's finance system to new software. Both were daunting tasks, but the opportunities for impact were immense.

However, even in my early days, the undercurrents within the organization were palpable. There was a pervasive fear among the expats that my arrival signaled an era of cuts and streamlining, a perception that would soon exacerbate tensions.

One of my first priorities was to address the lingering issue of foreign exchange reconciliation. Transactions spanning two years were scrutinized and balanced. After months of painstaking work, I reconciled the data and identified the discrepancies as historical. I sought the CEO's guidance on passing the necessary profit-and-loss entries, but Gade's response was evasive. He assured me that he would handle it.

Simultaneously, I turned my attention to the finance software migration. The vendor responsible for the implementation struggled to generate a basic balance sheet that matched our records. After several rounds of iterations and discussions, I uncovered a startling fact: the software was designed for manufacturing firms, not banks. I shared my assessment with the CEO, but was directed to ensure necessary amendments are carried out without any further delay, given this was mandated by the board.

As COO, my responsibilities expanded beyond the original mandate. Additional activities, such as bank guarantees and credit operations, were handed over to me. Upon reviewing these functions, I was shocked by the extent of the operational mess. Guarantees issued did not reconcile with the balance sheet, and errors in loan terms and interest rates were rampant.

For instance, a corporate loan with an agreed interest rate of 15% had been recorded as 1.5%. A 12-month term was erroneously captured as 120 months. Collateral securities were either not assigned or inaccurately documented. These discrepancies were not mere clerical errors—they posed serious risks to the bank's financial stability.

I systematically addressed each issue, keeping the CEO updated on my findings and actions. However, the growing accountability I brought to the system seemed to unnerve some stakeholders.

As I delved deeper into the bank's operations, I also noticed a troubling pattern. Customers were being instigated to lodge complaints with the directors. Given the close ties between the board members and the clientele, this was a calculated move to undermine my position.

The tension culminated at a board meeting in January. I was summoned to address concerns about my progress on the projects. The grilling was intense, but I requested the opportunity to present my six months of work.

When the board allowed me to speak, I laid out my activities systematically and without bias. I demonstrated how the reconciliation process was complete from my end and highlighted that the delay was due to the CEO's confirmation that he would be passing the adjustment entries. Regarding the software migration, I reiterated my recommendation to discontinue migration to the unsuitable system. The board accepted my suggestions, and I sensed that they would take up the matter with the CEO.

The board's decision did not sit well with Gade. He began to perceive me as a threat to his authority. While I had no intention of encroaching on his role, the divide between us deepened.

In the midst of these professional triumphs and growing hostility, I faced personal loss. Within a short span, both of my parents passed away. The grief of losing them, coupled with the inability to travel due to a lack of weekend flights, left me in a state of emotional turmoil. While I was away, the complaints against me intensified. By the time I returned, the environment had turned toxic.

The sadness began to affect my health, both physically and mentally. I was questioning whether the work environment, which had become toxic in certain areas, was worth the toll it was taking on me.

I realized that I had become a mercenary—working tirelessly but disconnected from the purpose and joy that once fueled my professional journey.

My wife, ever supportive, encouraged me to prioritize my well-being. After much reflection, I decided to resign, choosing to focus on my health and happiness over the demands of a job that had become emotionally draining. It was a moment of reckoning. I made the difficult decision to resign and return to India, prioritizing my health and peace of mind over the relentless grind.

A Farewell to Remember

When my resignation was accepted, it was immediate, bypassing the six-month notice period outlined in my contract. On my last day at Capital Bank, I was preparing to leave quietly, but Neo and Kagiso had other plans. They gathered the entire staff, except for the expatriate managers, in the banking hall to give me a heartfelt farewell.

In the midst of the speeches and emotional goodbyes, Neo, one of my most trusted colleagues, said, "We all know why you are leaving. Please stay back. We'll speak to the President of Botswana to keep you here. The country needs you."

While I politely declined their offer, I was moved by their sincerity and admiration. Their words reaffirmed what I had known all along: true leadership is about connecting with people and making a difference in their lives, no matter the challenges.

Months later, Gade visited India on vacation and reached out to me. To my surprise, he visited my home for dinner and offered a heartfelt apology. He admitted that he had been wrong and that together, we could have achieved remarkable transformations at the bank.

While I harbored no anger towards him, his words underscored the missed opportunities caused by ego and mistrust. The experience left me with valuable lessons about navigating organizational dynamics, the importance of integrity, and the resilience required to stand firm in the face of adversity.

The Legacy Left Behind

As I left Capital Bank, I reflected on the journey I had taken—from a skeptical and reserved team to a well-functioning unit that had embraced change and collaboration. It wasn't just about implementing processes or solving operational issues; it was about empowering people, building trust, and leaving a lasting impact.

Ten years have passed since that chapter of my life, and I still stay in touch with my Setswana family from Capital Bank. Their lives have moved forward, but the lessons we shared remain. My stint at Capital Bank was as transformative as it was tumultuous. It tested my professional acumen, emotional strength, and ability to lead under pressure. While the challenges were many, the experience enriched me with insights that have since shaped my approach as a coach and leader.

Looking back, I don't see it as a period of conflict but as a chapter of immense learning, a testament to the fact that even in the face of adversity, one can emerge stronger and wiser. After leaving, I took a much-needed sabbatical to recuperate, both physically and emotionally. That pause in my career would soon lead me to unexpected twists and turns.

CHAPTER 11

The Unfolding of New Opportunities

It was March 2014 when I received a call from my friend. He had joined CRISIL as President of SME Ratings and was looking for someone to streamline operations. A conversation over coffee turned into an opportunity, and I was soon onboard as Director of Operations.

CRISIL was a new challenge, a refreshing environment to apply my skills and build on my experience. I dived straight into understanding processes and identifying bottlenecks. The days were long but invigorating. Then, on my very first day at CRISIL, the phone rang.

The call was from Amit, an old acquaintance from my Botswana days. Amit had been our IT service provider at Capital Bank. At the time, I was ruthless in ensuring our vendors delivered to the highest standards. Amit's organization had been no exception, and my relentless demands had turned Capital Bank into a tough but rewarding client for him.

Back in those days, when Amit's team struggled to meet our requirements, he flew down to Botswana to sort things out personally. I still remember our first meeting. After hours of intense discussions in the office, I casually asked him about his evening plans. Amit hesitated, clearly trying to avoid spending more time with me after the day's grilling. Amused but understanding, I insisted he join me for dinner at my place.

That evening, over beers, we talked not just about work but also about life. By the time we dropped him off at his hotel, the ice had thawed. The very next morning, Amit presented a freshly drafted Service Level Agreement (SLA) that aligned perfectly with our expectations. From that point on, the partnership flourished.

Fast forward to 2014, and Amit's call wasn't just a friendly check-in. He had a proposal. One of his clients in Mauritius, a bank within the Bramer Group, was in urgent need of a Chief Operating Officer. Amit had recommended me for the role.

The timing was intriguing. I had just stepped into my role at CRISIL and was fully engrossed in understanding the business. Still, the opportunity was worth exploring. I informed Sachin about the conversation, and he encouraged me to pursue it.

Amit explained that while he had recommended me, the selection process would require me to apply formally. I sent in my application, and two weeks later, I was on a call with the Group CEO of Bramer Group. The interview went well, and he mentioned that I would be called for a second round.

But then, silence. Weeks passed, and no call came. I assumed the process had stalled or that the group had chosen another candidate. Rather than dwell on it, I threw myself into my work at CRISIL.

While the opportunity in Mauritius remained uncertain, the mere act of being considered was a reminder of how far my career had brought me. Amit's gesture of recommending me was rooted in the professional bond we had built years earlier.

For now, CRISIL kept me busy, but the possibilities that lay ahead had planted a seed of curiosity and ambition. What seemed like a regular day had turned into another chapter waiting to unfold.

Life at CRISIL was a paradox in motion. Work pressure was cyclical, like the waxing and waning of the moon, but much less poetic. The last week of every month, the office resembled a battlefield. The coffee machine worked overtime, employees clocked in 18-hour days, and survival instincts kicked in. But as soon as the first five days of the new month passed, the activity levels dropped after the month-end pressure eased.

The problem was evident: the sales pipeline was as inconsistent as monsoon rains, sales and operations were forever at odds, and the operations and credit assessment teams couldn't agree on anything except their mutual disdain for each other. Finance? They were the relentless hunters, chasing receivables like bloodhounds. If there was one thing we all excelled at, it was Excel sheets—pivot tables were practically our love language.

One day, I decided enough was enough. Armed with Business Head's buy in, and a hefty dose of caffeine, we launched a project to revisit timelines and cycles. In just three months, the transformation was remarkable. Month-end activities now wrapped up by 10 p.m., business revenues surged, and rating timelines shrank like an overcooked shirt. The cherry on top? I was received a Exemplary Leadership award.

While I was still basking in this unexpected recognition, July arrived, and with it, a twist I didn't see coming. One morning, I received a call from the CEO of the Bramer Group, who was in Mumbai with a bank chairman. He wanted to meet. I thought, "Sure, why not?" assuming it was a courtesy call. The meeting turned into a two-hour discussion that felt more like an impromptu interview. As I stood to leave, he asked the unexpected: "When can you join?"

I laughed nervously, thinking he was joking. He wasn't.

Barely a week later, I received another mysterious call from a lady. This time, the Group Chairman himself wanted to meet. The meeting was scheduled for 7 a.m. at the Taj Mahal Hotel. Who schedules a meeting at 7 a.m.? Bankers, apparently. The conversation was equally cryptic, and I left more puzzled than ever about what was in store.

Just as I'd resigned myself to focusing on my day-to-day work at CRISIL, an email landed in my personal inbox, followed swiftly by a call from Priscilla, Bramer Bank's HR head. She wanted me to fly to Mauritius to meet the board. Mauritius? Suddenly, my life felt like a Bollywood movie, complete with exotic locales and unexpected plot twists.

"I will take your blood."

Landing at SSR International airport at 6 a.m., I was out by 7:30 a.m., only to be whisked off to... Apollo Hospital?

Priscilla greeted me warmly and explained that I needed to undergo medical tests. Amused and mildly suspicious, I followed her lead. The nurse greeted me with, "Mr. Anil, I will take your blood now."

Take my blood? Was this a job offer or a vampire initiation?

After being poked, prodded, and scanned in every way imaginable, I was finally released by noon. Exhausted but desperate for caffeine, I managed to grab a quick coffee at the hotel before Priscilla called again. "The management team is waiting," she said cheerfully. I dashed out, leaving Anju, my ever-patient wife, to fend for herself.

At the head office, I was ushered into a huge meeting room and introduced to what felt like the entire executive team. They greeted me warmly, spoke enthusiastically about their vision, and outlined ambitious plans. One problem: no one had explicitly told me I'd been hired.

Confused but playing along, I nodded, smiled, and contributed just enough to avoid looking clueless. Back at the hotel, I thought I'd finally have time to catch my breath. But no. Lunch was followed by news of a board meeting at 4 p.m. However, since I was "running behind schedule," it was postponed to the next day.

Priscilla, ever the efficient host, then informed me we had cocktails and dinner at 7 p.m. The evening was a blur of introductions, toasts, and conversations. By the time we wrapped up at 10 p.m., I was both exhausted and exhilarated.

As I lay in bed that night, the whirlwind of the past few weeks replayed in my mind. From the chaos of CRISIL to the surreal experience of being courted by Bramer Bank, life had taken a turn I hadn't anticipated. What lay ahead? I wasn't sure. But one thing was certain: it was going to be an adventure.

CHAPTER 12

The Indian Odyssey to Mauritius: A Tale of Diaspora and Heritage

The boardroom at Ebene, perched on the 8th floor of the stunning Bramer House, was a sight to behold. As I stepped into the room, I couldn't help but take a moment to appreciate the breathtaking hill view outside the glass walls. The gentle hues of green against the Mauritian sky felt more like a luxurious painting than real life. The room itself was equally impressive, with a polished teak wooden table that seemed to stretch forever and leather chairs so plush that they practically begged you to stay a while.

It wasn't just picturesque; it was intimidating. My enthusiasm to make an impression at this meeting clashed briefly with a tinge of nervousness. After all, board meetings weren't exactly casual gatherings, and this one promised to be significant. The chairman began with a warm welcome, setting a tone that was simultaneously formal and friendly.

Then came my turn.

I was to give a small speech. "Small"—such a deceptive word. My version of small might be vastly different from theirs. Nevertheless, I rose to the occasion, quite literally, and began speaking. With each sentence, I tried to balance my enthusiasm and cheerful demeanor with the gravitas of the setting.

"...It is an honor to be considered for this opportunity, and I am excited about what we can achieve together," I concluded, feeling a mixture of relief and satisfaction.

The room was quiet for a moment. And then, to my surprise, one of the board members leaned forward and asked, "So, how soon can you join?"

The question caught me off guard. Wasn't this supposed to be a discussion? Maybe a follow-up interview? The final decision should've come after layers of deliberation and debate. Instead, they were ready to finalize things on the spot.

I blinked, smiled politely, and asked, "When do you want me to join?"

The room erupted in laughter, though I hadn't intended to crack a joke. Sensing my confusion, Priscilla, the HR representative, stepped in to manage the situation. She assured me that they were impressed with my credentials and enthusiasm, and they would work out the logistics quickly.

With that, the meeting wrapped up. I was still processing the whirlwind of events when I returned to my hotel. Not an hour later, Priscilla called me, her voice brimming with cheer. "We're sending over the offer letter soon," she said.

"Great!" I replied, although I felt a nagging sense that this was moving too fast.

Then came the bombshell. "We'll also need you to fill out some forms for the Mauritian banking regulators. It's just a formality."

Forms? Approvals? Banking regulators? This was beginning to sound less like a job offer and more like applying for a government clearance. Nevertheless, I couldn't say no. Mauritius was too beautiful, the offer too enticing.

But the surprises weren't over yet.

Late evening, the CEO called me personally. I assumed it was about salary negotiations, but apparently, that was a topic they had skipped entirely. Either they took me for granted, or they assumed I'd be too enchanted by the island to care.

"Just one thing," he began. "There's been a slight mix-up."

I stiffened. A mix-up? Had they changed their minds?

"There's no flight back to Mumbai tomorrow. The next one is in two days."

"Two days?" I echoed, my mind racing.

"Yes. Don't worry, we've arranged a city tour and some sightseeing for you. Consider it an unplanned vacation!"

Unplanned and unexpected honeymoon, more like. But what could I do? Declining their hospitality would've seemed ungrateful, and honestly, I didn't mind exploring Mauritius a little more.

The next two days were surreal. I toured the stunning beaches, the colonial architecture, and the vibrant local markets. Every moment felt like a postcard coming to life. By the time I finally boarded the plane back to Mumbai, I felt as if I'd already started my new life in Mauritius.

But the real adventure was yet to begin.

The regulatory approval process turned out to be far more labyrinthine than I had anticipated. What Priscilla had described as "just a formality" became a month-long odyssey involving endless paperwork, background checks, and a level of bureaucracy that would've impressed even Kafka.

During that time, I bid goodbye to CRISIL. Although my stint there had been relatively short, just eight months, I left with a sense of pride, knowing I'd made an impact. My colleagues gave me a warm send-off, complete with heartfelt speeches and a cake that was almost too beautiful to eat.

Finally, on October 15, I landed in Mauritius to join Bramer Bank. The island greeted me with its usual charm—bright skies, turquoise waters, and the kind of warmth that makes you forget the complexities of life.

My first day at the bank was a whirlwind of introductions, onboarding, and learning the ropes. Everyone was incredibly welcoming, though there were a few raised eyebrows about the mix-up regarding my flight. It seemed the story had become an inside joke among the staff.

Mauritius quickly became home. The work was challenging but fulfilling, and the lifestyle was unparalleled. Every weekend felt like a mini-vacation, with beaches, hiking trails, and an endless array of seafood to explore.

Looking back, the whole journey—from the picturesque boardroom to the unplanned sightseeing tour—felt like a comedy of errors wrapped in an adventure. If there's one thing I've learned from the experience, it's that life has a way of throwing curveballs when you least expect them. And sometimes, those curveballs lead you to the most beautiful places, literally and figuratively.

Who needs an ordinary onboarding process when you can have a Mauritian honeymoon instead?

Mesmerizing Mauritius

Nestled in the azure waters of the Indian Ocean, Mauritius is often called paradise on Earth. Despite its modest size of just 2,040 square kilometers, this island nation boasts a rich blend of cultural diversity, historical significance, and economic vibrancy. Beyond its stunning beaches and luxury resorts lies a story of resilience, adaptation, and harmony—a story that draws expatriates and captivates newcomers with its unique cultural fusion and opportunities.

Mauritius is part of the Mascarene Islands, along with Réunion and Rodrigues. The island's landscape, dominated by lush mountains, volcanic cliffs, and expansive sugarcane fields, offers a striking contrast to its pristine coastline, framed by coral reefs and tranquil lagoons. These natural wonders not only attract tourists but also support key industries like agriculture and fishing.

The island's fame is partly due to the now-extinct dodo, a flightless bird endemic to Mauritius. Once a symbol of extinction, the dodo serves as a poignant reminder of the delicate balance between nature and human activity.

Mauritius' history is shaped by centuries of migration, colonization, and trade. Though uninhabited when Arab sailors discovered it in the 10th century, the Portuguese were the first Europeans to reach the island in the early 1500s. In 1598, the Dutch claimed Mauritius, introducing sugarcane but eventually abandoning it by 1710 due to harsh conditions.

The French arrived next, renaming it the Isle de France and establishing a prosperous colony with African slaves working on sugar plantations. Following the British conquest during the Napoleonic Wars, Mauritius became a British colony in 1810. The abolition of slavery in 1835 prompted the importation of indentured laborers from India, who brought with them languages, religions, and traditions. Mauritius gained independence in 1968 and became a republic in 1992.

In the mid-19th century, after slavery was abolished, Mauritius faced a labor shortage on its sugar estates. The French and British sought workers from India. The French brought laborers from Pondicherry, mostly Tamil and Telugu speakers, who endured grueling work in the sugarcane fields. The British, on the other hand, recruited from Bihar, sending skilled workers known as "coolies" to serve in transport and trade. Their Bhojpuri dialect and strong work ethic left an indelible mark on Mauritius' cultural and linguistic landscape.

Today, Mauritius is a vibrant fusion of Indian, African, European, and Chinese influences.

Mauritius is a rare example of how diversity can foster unity. Despite its multi-ethnic population, the island has cultivated a shared national identity rooted in mutual respect. Festivals like Diwali, Eid, Christmas, and Chinese New Year are celebrated with equal enthusiasm, reflecting the inclusive spirit of the island.

The Mauritian Creole language serves as a unifying force, while English and French are official languages. English dominates government and business, while French is more commonly spoken in daily life. This linguistic flexibility reflects the island's ability to adapt in a globalized world.

Mauritian cuisine is another testament to this cultural blend, with Indian curries, Chinese dim sum, French pastries, and Creole rougaille all contributing to a vibrant culinary scene. Local street markets offer everything from dholl puri to spicy fritters, making food a central part of the island's identity.

Tourism plays a vital role in the economy, drawing over a million visitors each year to its beaches, lagoons, and iconic attractions like the Seven Colored Earths. Adventure seekers can hike through Black River Gorges National Park or swim with dolphins in Tamarin Bay. Mauritius' strategic location has also made it a hub for financial services, attracting global businesses with its favorable tax regime and infrastructure.

One early challenge Indian immigrants faced was the colonial administrators' difficulty in pronouncing their names. Over time, these names were altered to suit the French or British tongue, resulting in unique Mauritian variations with Indian roots.

I recall meeting a man named Armoogum, whose ancestor hailed from Pondicherry. He laughed as he explained that his name had originally been Arumugam, meaning "six-faced" in reference to Lord Murugan. "The French made it easier for themselves," he chuckled. "Now even I can't imagine spelling it the Indian way!"

Despite these adaptations, Indo-Mauritians have maintained strong cultural ties to India, celebrating every major festival with fervor. Among them, Mahashivratri stands out as the most significant Hindu festival in Mauritius.

Every February, thousands of Hindus embark on a pilgrimage to Ganga Talao, a volcanic crater lake surrounded by lush greenery. Believed to be as sacred as the Ganges River, pilgrims carry holy water from the lake to offer to Lord Shiva. Dressed in white and saffron, devotees carry decorated kanwars on their shoulders, singing bhajans as they walk barefoot for miles. The sight is breathtaking—families camping by the roadside, conch shells and temple bells filling the air, and vendors offering food and drinks to the pilgrims. I'll never forget serving snacks at a stall with Anju, both of us wearing dark green Bramer Bank t-shirts, amidst the sea of devotion.

When the Volcano Sleeps

Rajen picked me up from our new home in Floreal. Nestled atop a volcanic hill, Floreal was a surreal locality, unlike any place I had lived before. Our gated community was a quiet haven surrounded by the lush greenery of Mauritius. Just a hundred meters away lay the iconic Trou aux Cerfs, a dormant volcanic crater that added an air of mystique to the landscape.

The crater, with its perfectly circular rim lined with dense vegetation, seemed to hold secrets of the island's geological past. From its edge, one could see panoramic views of the surrounding plains, towns, and even the turquoise waters of the Indian Ocean in the distance.

Our neighborhood was serene, with neat, winding streets flanked by trees and colorful gardens. Early mornings were a delight; the air was crisp, and the occasional chirping of birds provided a natural symphony. This peaceful setting felt like the perfect retreat after long days at work. As Rajen navigated the winding road down from Floreal, I couldn't help but feel grateful for this unique chapter of my life.

We headed towards Ebene, the business hub of Mauritius, where Bramer House stood tall. Known for its modern infrastructure, Ebene was a striking contrast to the rest of the island's more traditional charm. Bramer House was an architectural marvel, with its sleek design and reflective glass façade. It was a symbol of progress, ambition, and the hub of my new professional journey.

Stepping into my office for the first time, I was struck by its size and elegance. Originally designed as a reception area for private clients, it had been converted into my workspace. Its expansive windows allowed natural light to flood in, creating an environment that was both energizing and welcoming. The office symbolized the weight of the responsibility I had taken on.

My first official meeting was with the CEO. As we sat across from each other, he outlined his expectations with clarity and precision. The bank was at the forefront of the industry, but maintaining that position required innovation, agility, and leadership. His trust in me was evident, and I felt a deep sense of responsibility to deliver on his expectations.

Following this, I was introduced to the management team. It was a diverse group with a wealth of experience, each member bringing unique strengths to the table. During our initial meeting, I emphasized the importance of mutual trust and collaboration. My message was simple: I was here to support them, and in return, I needed their unwavering support as we navigated the challenges ahead.

My next task was to meet the heads of departments individually. These were key players who drove the bank's operational success. I asked them a simple yet profound question:

What does your department need to be the best at, and why?

It was a question that required introspection and strategic thinking. I gave them a week to reflect and provide actionable responses. This exercise wasn't just about identifying gaps; it was about fostering a mindset of excellence and accountability. By the end of these meetings, I had a clear roadmap of deliverables and a sense of where we stood as an organization.

Understanding the work culture was my next priority. The HR team provided me with a detailed overview, highlighting the bank's strengths and areas for improvement. But I wanted more than just reports; I wanted firsthand experience. That's when the idea of "2 by 10" struck me.

Every morning at 9 a.m., I invited two randomly selected staff members from different departments to my office for a cup of tea. The conversations were informal, focusing on their lives outside work—their families, hobbies, aspirations, and challenges. These chats offered me a window into their world, helping me understand what motivated them and what held them back.

At the end of each session, I asked two questions:

- What support do you need from me to become better than you are today?
- What support can you provide me to make Bramer Bank the best bank in Mauritius?

These conversations became a cornerstone of my leadership approach. Over the next four months, I met every single staff member. People who had never ventured onto the management floor now felt seen and valued. For many, it was a moment of recognition, an opportunity to be heard by someone at the top.

The impact was transformative. Service levels improved dramatically, turnaround times reduced, and customer complaints became rare. But perhaps the most significant change was in the workplace culture. Inter-departmental conflicts diminished, replaced by a spirit of camaraderie and mutual respect. People started knowing each other beyond their job titles, fostering a sense of unity.

Simultaneously, I made it a point to visit one branch every day. These visits allowed me to connect with branch staff and managers, gaining insights into their challenges and strengths. It also reinforced the message that every part of the organization was equally important.

As the months passed, the results were undeniable. Bramer Bank was thriving. The cultural shift was evident, and the organization felt like a well-oiled machine. I was fortunate to have the support of capable colleagues. Priscilla, a key member of my team, was both a friend and a pillar of strength. Her sudden announcement that she was moving on to better opportunities was a shock. While I would miss her, I respected her decision.

Steve, her successor, was an ex-HSBC professional with a sharp mind and a collaborative approach. We hit it off immediately. Another ally was Ramesh, the head of risk. His calm demeanor and pragmatic outlook made him a confidant during difficult times.

Six months into my tenure, the external landscape began to change. A new government had come to power, bringing with it an air of uncertainty. Initially, we stayed focused, confident in our resilience. But then came the unthinkable. Late one evening, we received news that our banking license had been suspended due to liquidity issues.

The atmosphere in the office shifted overnight. What had been a bustling, optimistic environment now felt heavy with anxiety and disbelief. As the only expatriate in the leadership team, I sought guidance from our High Commission. Their advice was clear: given the unfolding situation, I should consider relocating to my home country immediately.

Flight to Freedom

As I packed up my belongings, I reflected on the journey. The volcanic crater at Floreal came to mind—a symbol of calm and strength, yet a reminder of nature's unpredictability. My time at Bramer Bank had been much the same.

In just a few months, we had achieved remarkable progress. The "2 by 10" initiative had transformed the organization, creating a culture of trust and collaboration. Service excellence had become the norm, and our turnaround times were benchmarks for others to follow. Yet, external forces beyond our control had brought this chapter to an abrupt end.

What stayed with me was the resilience and spirit of the people. The bonds we had forged, the cultural shift we had achieved, and the progress we had made were not erased by this setback.

Leadership, I realized, is not about the title or the office. It is about the connections you build, the trust you inspire, and the change you drive. It is about empowering others to rise to their potential and fostering a culture where excellence becomes second nature.

Sitting on the aircraft flying back home, the weight of the past six months bore down on me. Mauritius had become a second home—a place of new beginnings, challenges, and triumphs. Yet, the abrupt suspension of the bank's license had upended everything. The situation felt surreal, like the calm crater at Trou aux Cerfs suddenly erupting with turmoil.

I couldn't help but ask myself: Should I have left the bank so quickly? What if I had stayed back?

The questions lingered. I had poured my heart and soul into Bramer Bank, building a culture of collaboration and trust. Walking away from this wasn't just about leaving a job; it felt like leaving behind a part of myself. I thought of the staff who had confided in me during our "2 by 10" sessions, their faces filled with hope and a sense of belonging. Many of them had never been recognized before, and now they were beginning to see themselves as contributors to something larger. What would my departure signal to them?

Yet, the realities of the situation were harsh. The bank was no longer in control of its destiny; it was under siege. The government had stepped in, taking over operations to stabilize the financial system. The high commission's advice weighed heavily on me. I was an expatriate in an alien country, and the situation was volatile. Their recommendation to leave was pragmatic, but the emotional toll of that decision was enormous.

Was My Decision to Leave the Rght One?

In the days that followed, I kept replaying the what-ifs in my mind. What if I had stayed? Could I have helped navigate the crisis, offering leadership and reassurance to the team? I knew I had earned their trust and respect, and perhaps my presence could have been a stabilizing force. But then again, there were limits to what I could have achieved. The suspension of the license wasn't a matter of internal management; it was the result of external forces that were far beyond my control.

I had to face the uncomfortable truth that no amount of effort or goodwill could have prevented the crisis. Staying might have delayed the inevitable—or worse, entangled me in a situation where I could do little but watch the institution crumble from within. And yet, walking away still felt like an unfinished chapter, a narrative cut short before its resolution.

What Would I Do Differently if Faced with a Similar Situation Again?

For one, I would lean even more heavily on the power of connection. The relationships I had built—whether through the "2 by 10" initiative, branch visits, or leadership interactions—had been my greatest strength. They had provided not only insights but also a wellspring of trust and goodwill that carried us through difficult times.

Second, I would ensure that contingency plans were more robust, both personally and professionally. As a leader, you must be prepared for crises, but as an expatriate, you must also think about your own safety and stability. Balancing these priorities is not easy, but it is essential.

And finally, I would remind myself that leadership is about creating lasting value, even if you are not there to see it fully realized. The cultural shift we had achieved at Bramer Bank was something no external crisis could erase. The seeds of collaboration, trust, and empowerment had been planted, and I trusted they would continue to bear fruit long after I had left.

As we climbed higher, the island disappeared from view, but its impact on me remained vivid. Mauritius had taught me resilience in the face of uncertainty, the power of human connection, and the importance of knowing when to hold on—and when to let go.

04

THE SEARCH FOR MEANING

CHAPTER 13

The Void Years – When Success Felt Hollow

The Spotlight — and the Exit

Mauritius was a professional high point. I had taken on a significant leadership role with wide visibility. The pace was steady, the mandate clear, and the transformation work meaningful. I found myself in the media, quoted in business coverage, and recognised as a face of change. People even began to recognise me in public.

For a while, it felt energising. As someone who had spent decades in the trenches, it was affirming to finally be seen, I told myself I had earned it.

But then came the news: the bank was closing. Due to reasons outside my control, regulatory and reputational, the institution I had helped shape was being wound down.

There was no exit strategy. No transition plan. Just the end of something I had poured myself into. Just a finality that came too quickly.

I had faced many endings in my career. But this was different. This one was beyond my control.

I packed my things. Shook hands. Smiled. Inside, I felt disoriented. Like a chapter had ended without resolution.

And the timing made it more complex. I had already transitioned through four demanding roles after leaving HSBC — each time adapting, realigning, rebuilding. Mauritius had felt like a landing zone. Stable, valuable, recognised.

But now it was gone.

On the flight back, I stared at the clouds and thought: How did I go from centre-stage to complete stillness in a matter of weeks? Did I anchor myself too deeply in something I could not control?

That moment didn't break me. But it cracked something open. For the first time in years, I felt adrift, not because I failed, but because the foundation I had stood on was taken away. I wasn't sure what I was going back to or what came next.

When the Map No Longer Matches the Terrain

The old playbook had always worked: deliver results, earn trust, build momentum. It had taken me across countries and into senior roles.

When I joined a startup after leaving Mauritius, I expected a new kind of challenge: fast-paced, agile, with room to build. And it was, but something felt different, and not in a good way.

The role looked right on paper — strategy, growth, people. But I found myself going through the motions. I was doing everything I was supposed to, yet it felt like I was watching someone else do it. Meetings blurred into each other. The energy that used to come naturally now had to be summoned. I had built my career on clarity and confidence. But here, I was often questioning what I was doing and why I wasn't fully in it.

The people were good. The opportunity was real. But I didn't feel rooted. That's when I realised something had shifted; not in the organisation, but in me. I was trying to apply an old formula to a new phase of life. The terrain had changed. And my map was outdated.

The Performance Trap

The startup was full of promise, with new product lines, investor interest, and scale potential. I was brought in to add structure and strategic clarity. But very soon, I noticed I was slipping into an old pattern. I became the reliable one. The composed one. The one who could handle ambiguity and make decisions without fuss.

At first, it felt like I was contributing meaningfully. But over time, it began to feel like I was performing.

In one meeting, I was giving feedback to a younger team — calmly, clearly — but inside I felt completely detached. Not from them, but from myself. I had done this a thousand times before. The words came, the leadership tone was there, but the connection wasn't.

I smiled when I didn't feel like it. Said "Let's go" when I felt like pausing. This wasn't a burnout. I had the energy, but I didn't have the emotional investment.

And that's when it hit me: I was not just managing teams. I was managing my own lack of engagement. That's a different kind of pressure, and one that no designation can fix.

The Strange Quiet After the Applause

There's something surreal about seeing your name in print. The first time it had happened in Mauritius, I bought two copies of the Business Magazine: one for keeps, one to send home. A part of me felt like I had arrived.

But it didn't last. In the months after my exit, I stumbled upon one of those old articles. It was a glowing feature on my leadership style and strategic vision. I reread it and it felt like I was reading about someone else. Detached. Distant. Like looking at a suit I once wore that no longer fit.

The applause had stopped. But more importantly, I realised I no longer needed it. That was the oddest part. Recognition is a powerful thing. But over time, if it doesn't land on something solid inside you, it just echoes.

I had come to associate external validation with internal value. And now, with the recognition gone, I was forced to ask: Who am I without the articles, the interviews, the LinkedIn applause? The silence that followed wasn't empty. It was instructive.

I began to understand that applause is temporary, but alignment is enduring. What mattered now wasn't whether people still remembered my name. What mattered was whether I remembered who I wanted to become.

The Questions That Don't Go Away

It all started subtly. First a pause before a meeting. A sigh before logging on. A thought left unfinished in the middle of a conversation. Then, questions began to form.

Why am I doing this? Who am I becoming through this work? Would I choose this life again if I had no one to impress?

I didn't have answers. But the questions didn't stop. They showed up in unexpected places — in the silence of early mornings, during commutes, over solo lunches. They were not dramatic or urgent. Just steady. Like water carving through rock.

Some days, I dismissed them as fatigue. Other days, I feared them. Because these weren't logistical questions, they were existential ones. Not "How do I fix this?" but "What does this mean now?" And once those kinds of questions enter your inner dialogue, they don't leave until they're addressed.

I tried journaling. Walking more. Talking less. But mostly, I just sat with discomfort. For someone who had always been sure, always moving, always achieving, this space of not knowing was deeply unfamiliar. And yet, something inside me whispered: Stay here. Don't rush. There's something here for you.

During that phase, I began noticing a shift; not just at work, but at home.

The startup had taken a lot out of me. Not in terms of hours — I had worked harder elsewhere — but in terms of meaning. That same energy followed me home.

I realised I had developed a habit of partial presence. I was physically available, but not emotionally tuned in.

And the people closest to us don't care about our outputs. They feel our presence. Or lack of it.

That realization hurt. Because I always prided myself on being grounded. Reliable. Engaged.

But I had become someone who appeared composed — yet was quietly unraveling beneath the surface.

The hardest part was that I couldn't explain what I was feeling, even to myself. I wasn't struggling. I wasn't unhappy. But I wasn't fully me either.

I had always worn many hats — leader, advisor, mentor, builder. Over the years, those roles had started overlapping. Eventually, they began to blur. In the startup, I found myself constantly switching gears between product, people, process, and performance. It was exhilarating in theory, but in practice, it left little space for reflection.

I was effective, sure. But I had stopped being authentic. The lines between role and self had become too thin. I could still lead with clarity. But I no longer felt deeply anchored in why I was leading. And that's a dangerous place to be — where your actions are intact, but your intentions are hollow.

You're still functioning. You still show up. But there's a growing distance between your performance and your personality. I was just misaligned. And I had gone too long without noticing.

So I kept myself busy, relentlessly. Planning strategy, refining processes, advising founders, firefighting issues. All that, to avoid thinking.

As long as I stayed engaged, I didn't have to ask the uncomfortable question: Is this what I want anymore?

That's the thing about busyness: it's respectable and admirable. People see you as driven, productive, dependable. But for me, it had quietly become a disguise. A way to mask the fog I was carrying inside.

On weekends, I'd open the laptop even when I didn't need to. Not because of urgency, but because silence had become harder to sit with. I was afraid of stillness. Because in stillness, I might have to admit that I was successful but not fulfilled. And that scared me.

So I worked harder. Until even that stopped working.

Some people speak of sudden breakdowns. For me, it came differently — as a low, persistent hum. A quiet inner agitation. It didn't shout. It nudged. It was there during long drives. It hovered in early morning silences. It lingered after I closed yet another tab of work.

I didn't need more success. I needed to feel alive in my own work again.

But I didn't know how to find my way back. Not yet.

The Truth That Found Me

Eventually, I stopped running.

One Sunday morning, I was sipping tea on the balcony, no emails, no calls, and I finally admitted to myself: I'm not okay. And that's okay.

It wasn't a breakdown. Just an honest check-in.

For years, I had led with strength. And now, I needed to lead with truth. The void I felt wasn't a crisis. It was a message. A signal that something deeper was waiting to emerge.

I didn't need to quit everything. I didn't need to burn it all down. I just needed to stop lying to myself that "this is fine." Because it wasn't; and in that quiet acknowledgement, something shifted.

The fog didn't lift immediately. But I felt lighter. More honest. More awake. That moment gave me the courage to begin listening to myself again. I had spent decades building – building systems, teams, results. Now, it was time to build something inward.

That's where this next chapter really began — not with action, but with admission. That I was no longer the man I used to be. And that maybe, just maybe, that was a good thing.

CHAPTER 14

Family: My Anchors, My Wings

Anju: The Heart of My Story

The year was 1988, and my life felt like a turbulent ocean, uncertain waves of ambition crashing into the shores of doubt. Enter Anju, a teacher with a calm demeanor and a smile that hinted at an unshakable strength. She didn't just step into my life; she became the lighthouse guiding me through its storms.

Our wedding was a modest affair, a blend of rituals, laughter, and a touch of chaos in the chilly winters of December. While I trembled and fumbled through the ceremonies, Anju stood poised, as if she had already rehearsed this role a thousand times. Friends teased me about marrying a teacher— "Now you'll always have homework!" they joked. Little did I realize, the greatest lessons of my life would come from her.

Navigating her role as a daughter-in-law was another chapter in Anju's story of quiet resilience. My mother, a strong-willed matriarch, being a military officer's wife, had her own way of running the household. Anju, with her tact and patience, managed to earn her respect while maintaining her individuality.

There were moments of tension, of course. I remember one time when my mother critiqued Anju's cooking—an almost sacred battleground in Indian households. Anju, instead of taking offense, turned it into a learning moment. "Teach me, Mum," she said with genuine interest. By the end of the session, they were laughing over stories from my childhood.

Anju's teaching career was not just a job—it was her passion. She loved shaping young minds, and her students adored her.

Anju's journey as a mother was nothing short of heroic. From late-night fevers to school projects, she handled it all with unwavering dedication. Our children grew up in a home filled with love, learning, and a touch of mischief.

One memory stands out. Our daughter, then 4 years old, had scribbled on the living room wall with crayons. I expected an explosion of anger, but Anju surprised me. She handed him a cloth and said, "Let's clean it together." Later, she turned to me and added with a wink, "If you ever feel like expressing yourself, please use washable markers."

We started our married life in New Delhi, full of dreams and aspirations. One of our first milestones was buying a house there, a testament to our shared vision of building a stable and secure future. However, life had other plans. In 1996, my career took us to Mumbai, and that house in Delhi became a symbol of what we left behind to chase new opportunities.

But when I had to relocate to Mumbai, she chose to step away from the classroom. This decision was neither easy nor forced; it was simply her way of prioritizing what mattered most to her—family.

Leaving her career behind was a sacrifice I didn't fully grasp until much later. She became the full-time educator for our children, weaving learning into everyday moments. "Who needs a school," she'd joke, "when the teacher lives at home?"

Mumbai: The Maximum City with Maximum Challenges

Settling in Mumbai was no small feat. Known as the city that never sleeps, it came with its own set of challenges, especially for a young family uprooted from the familiarity of Delhi. My work demanded long hours and extensive travel, leaving Anju to manage the home front almost single-handedly.

The children were still young, and their schooling became a logistical challenge. Mumbai's relentless monsoons, combined with the city's chaotic traffic, made ferrying the kids to school a daily battle. Yet, come rain or shine, Anju ensured they never missed a day.

Her determination to provide the children with a sense of normalcy despite the chaos was awe-inspiring. Our small apartment in Mumbai may not have been grand, but Anju's touch made it a warm and welcoming haven, a place where the noise of the city faded into laughter and love.

My work in Mumbai consumed most of my waking hours. There were days when I'd leave at sunrise and return well after the children were asleep. It was a sacrifice I had to make, but the guilt of being an absent father and husband weighed heavily on me.

Anju, however, never once complained. She shouldered the emotional and physical labor of keeping the family running, all while ensuring I had the peace of mind to focus on my career. Her strength became my refuge, and her belief in me became the fuel that kept me going.

Looking back, our years in Mumbai were among the most challenging, yet they were also transformative. It was during this time that I truly began to understand the depth of Anju's resilience. She didn't just adapt to the city's demands—she thrived, turning every challenge into an opportunity to grow, both as a mother and as a partner.

Her sacrifices during those years laid the foundation for everything that came afterward, setting the tone for the life we would build together.

The Bangalore Challenge: Separation and Strength

In 1999, I moved to Bangalore while Anju and the children had to stay behind in Delhi due to logistical challenges. It wasn't easy for Anju to manage two young children. There were days when the loneliness gnawed at her, but she never let it show. I recall one particular conversation when I apologized for being away. She simply said, "Don't worry about us. Just make sure you're giving your best there—it'll all be worth it."

Her words carried a determination that shamed my guilt and inspired me to push harder. She created a cocoon of normalcy for our children, shielding them from the challenges of a fragmented family life. While I was miles away, chasing career goals, she ensured our family didn't just survive but thrived.

Later, I got transferred back to Mumbai in 2000.

Starting Anew: Botswana and Beyond

Our move to Botswana in 2012 marked a turning point in our lives. It was a world away from the comfort zones we had known—a different culture, a new environment, and the challenge of building a life from scratch. I still remember the day we landed. The vast, open skies of Gaborone greeted us, but so did the uncertainty of starting anew.

Anju, however, was undaunted. She approached the situation with a quiet confidence, diving into the task of creating a home in a foreign land. The challenges were many—adapting to the local way of life, finding her footing in an unfamiliar social fabric—but she took it all in stride.

Her biggest trial was managing the transition while children remained in Mumbai due to higher education. She became their anchor, helping them adjust to a new way of life on their own, making them self-dependent. She personally embraced the cultural richness of Botswana. Despite the struggles, she found joy in the small things—visiting local markets, doing social work, forming new friendships, and discovering the dignity of labor that defined the local culture.

Mauritius came next, with its stunning beaches and vibrant expat community. While it was easier in some ways, Anju's role as the cornerstone of our family remained unchanged. She turned each house into a home, ensuring stability for us amidst the constant shifts of my career.

The Shoulder I Leaned On

Life threw its share of challenges our way. There were times when my professional journey hit roadblocks, moments when I doubted my abilities. Anju, however, never wavered. She became my confidante, my counselor, and my cheerleader.

I vividly remember one evening when I came home, overwhelmed by a setback at work. Sitting in the dark, I confided my fears to her. She listened patiently, then said, "Do you trust me?" I nodded. "Then trust this—we'll get through it together." Her words were a lifeline, pulling me out of despair.

Finding Humor in Chaos

Anju's sense of humor was also the glue that held our family together. She had a knack for turning even the most stressful situations into moments of laughter. Like the time I forgot our anniversary. I tried to cover it up with an impromptu dinner plan, only for Anju to quip, "Don't worry, I'll remind you next year. Same date, in case you're wondering."

Her humor extended to our parenting adventures as well. When our daughter went through a "why" phase, peppering us with endless questions, Anju responded with wit and creativity. "Why is the sky blue?" our daughter asked one day. "Because the sun got tired of yellow," Anju replied with a smile.

Finding My Purpose: Her Silent Contribution

One of the most profound aspects of Anju's support came during a period of personal transformation. After decades of climbing the corporate ladder, I began exploring my deeper purpose—transitioning into coaching, learning about NLP, and building a life centered on service and empowerment. It was an expensive journey, requiring not just time but significant financial investment.

Anju, without hesitation, dipped into her savings to support me. She believed in my vision even before I had fully articulated it. "This is for us," she said as she handed over the funds. "Your growth will be ours too."

Her faith in me was both humbling and motivating. Every certification, every milestone I achieved as a coach, carried her fingerprints. She didn't just fund my purpose; she made it her own.

A Legacy of Strength and Sacrifice

Today, as I look back on our life together, I am struck by the quiet power of Anju's sacrifices. Whether it was holding the family together during my absence in Bangalore, navigating the challenges of expat life in Botswana and Mauritius, or funding my dreams, she has been the invisible force behind every success I've ever known.

If there's one thing Anju has taught me, it's that love is not just about standing beside someone during the good times. It's about shouldering their burdens, believing in their dreams, and creating a foundation of strength and trust.

This chapter is my tribute to her—a woman who gave up so much so that I could become the man I am today. For the dreams you set aside, the battles you fought silently, and the love you gave unconditionally. You are the heart of our family, the reason our home is a sanctuary, and the quiet force behind every success I've ever known.

Anju, my anchor, my teacher, my unwavering partner, thank you for being the heart of our story.

Here's to you—the teacher who never stopped teaching, the mother who gave everything, and the wife who made life worth living.

A Father's Journey of Letting Go – Detached Attachment

In 2016, Rohan stood at a crossroads, a common enough place for a young man who had just completed his engineering degree. Yet, as his father, it felt momentous to me, a pivotal moment not just in his life but in ours as a family. His dilemma—whether to join the workforce or pursue a management degree—was as much a question of direction as it was of passion. And for someone as young as him, finding that elusive passion is never straightforward.

I wanted to help him decide, not by imposing my views but by guiding him to make his own informed choice. Over the years, I had shared countless stories about Puneet. Rohan admired Puneet from afar, not just for his professional achievements but also for his ability to find joy in life's simpler pleasures—his love for golf. In fact, Puneet had gifted Rohan a golf putter set on his birthday, a gesture that seemed to bridge the gap between generations.

While Rohan enjoyed practicing indoors with the golf putter, his true passion was music. Yet, passion doesn't always dictate one's career choices, and that is where the dilemma lay. To help him find clarity, I reached out to two trusted colleagues, Ravi Bajaj and Raman Ahuja. Both were engineers, much younger than me, and well-acquainted with the modern professional landscape. I believed that hearing their experiences and perspectives would provide Rohan with the insights he needed.

Both Ravi and Raman were kind enough to meet with Rohan. They answered his questions patiently, cleared his doubts, and shared the realities of engineering careers versus the opportunities a management degree might offer. Their guidance was invaluable, but ultimately, the decision was Rohan's to make. He did his own research, weighing the pros and cons, exploring his aspirations, and eventually deciding to pursue a Master's degree in the United States.

When he informed us that he had been accepted into Johns Hopkins University, I felt a mix of pride and apprehension. This was a remarkable achievement, a testament to his hard work and determination. Yet, the reality of him moving halfway across the world was hard to digest. As a parent, the thought of your child leaving home, possibly for good, is not an easy one. It wasn't just about the distance; it was about the unknown. Would he thrive in a new environment? Would he be happy? Would he remember to call home?

My wife, too, was grappling with these questions, perhaps more intensely than I was. As mothers often do, she was worried about the practicalities—his safety, his ability to manage on his own, and whether he would eat properly. I found myself in the role of the rational parent, explaining to her why we needed to support his decision. "Our role is to give him wings," I told her. "Wings to fly, with the best education and strong values. We must trust that he will make the right choices."

Yet, even as I spoke those words, I couldn't shake off my own unease. The day of his departure seemed to approach at an alarming speed. To create some lasting memories before he left, we planned a short family vacation to Malaysia. It was a beautiful trip, yet I found myself distracted, observing Rohan more than engaging with him. I watched him laugh, joke, and explore, all the while thinking about the void his absence would create in our lives.

The departure date—August 15, 2017—finally arrived. It was India's Independence Day, a date steeped in symbolism, and I jokingly told Rohan, "You're getting your independence today." He laughed, but I knew he understood the weight of the moment. At the airport, we exchanged our goodbyes, and I hugged him tighter than usual, trying to hold onto the boy who had grown up far too quickly.

The days and weeks after he left were an adjustment, to say the least. The house felt quieter, emptier. I found myself glancing at his room out of habit, expecting to see him hunched over his laptop or strumming his guitar. Conversations with him shifted to phone calls and video chats, and while it was reassuring to see him thrive in his new environment, it wasn't the same as having him home.

Rohan flourished at Johns Hopkins. He worked hard, made friends, and immersed himself in the opportunities that came his way. As parents, we supported him wholeheartedly, even as the years went by and the reality of his absence settled into our lives. It's been seven years now, and he has built a life for himself in the United States—a life that we are incredibly proud of, but also one that keeps him far from home. He is a good golfer too, having recently bought his new golf set.

As I reflect on those early days of his departure, I realize how much I learned as a father during that time. Letting go of your child is one of the hardest things to do, but it is also one of the most important. It is a test of faith—faith in the values you've instilled, faith in their ability to navigate the world, and faith in the bond that distance can never weaken.

Even now, I occasionally find myself reminiscing about the years when Rohan was home, when our lives revolved around his school schedules, his hobbies, and his dreams. But I also take comfort in knowing that we gave him the foundation to build a life he loves. And while I may jokingly call August 15 his "Independence Day," I know that his success is also our shared triumph, a testament to the love, support, and belief we placed in him.

A Daughter's Devotion to Family

Seeing Rohan off at the airport that day was a bittersweet moment. Our son, full of dreams and determination, was leaving for the United States to pursue his ambitions. Anju and I had decided beforehand that we would control our emotions, knowing how much this moment meant to him. Yet, when the time came, it was far harder than we had anticipated.

Anju had a particularly tough time. As much as she tried to keep her composure, the thought of Rohan being so far away overwhelmed her. I saw the tears welling up in her eyes, though she tried to hide them behind a brave smile. Her silence spoke volumes. She held his hand tightly, as if reluctant to let him go, but finally managed to whisper, "Take care of yourself, beta, and call us often."

I, too, struggled to hold back my emotions, but I knew I had to be the anchor in that moment. As Rohan waved goodbye and disappeared through the gates, the weight of his absence hit us both. It was Nidhi who stepped forward, offering quiet strength when we needed it most.

She gently placed her hand on mine, her voice trembling with a mix of empathy and determination. "I am with you. Calm down, please," she said, her eyes glistening with tears that mirrored ours. Then, unable to hold back, she started crying, and I held her close, grateful for her presence.

Nidhi had just begun her career in digital technology after completing her master's degree in management. Bright, ambitious, and with a strong sense of purpose, she had plans of her own. She had been working tirelessly toward her Canadian permanent residency (PR), having cleared the necessary tests and jumping through the many hoops of the application process. Yet, on that day, I sensed something deeper within her—a quiet resolve to stay close, to prioritize family over distant horizons.

It wasn't long before her path took a beautiful turn. Nidhi met Anish, a kind and thoughtful young man who shared her values and dreams. Love blossomed, and they decided to get married in 2021, after navigating the uncertainties of the pandemic. It was a joyous occasion, a celebration of not just their union but of hope and resilience during challenging times.

However, the journey toward her Canadian PR was far from smooth. The process, already known for its lengthy timelines, came to a standstill during the Covid emergency. Months turned into years, and just when Nidhi had almost put it out of her mind, the long-awaited approval arrived—a month after her wedding.

The Canadian consulate, upon noticing her updated marital status, required her to reapply, this time with Anish as her spouse. While some might have found this development frustrating, Nidhi and Anish approached it with patience and practicality. By 2022, they both received their PR approval, an achievement that marked the culmination of years of effort and persistence.

Yet, as the saying goes, life is what happens while you're busy making other plans. By this time, five years had passed since Rohan had left for the U.S., and our family's priorities had shifted. Nidhi and Anish had grown deeply rooted in their lives here, finding fulfillment in their work, relationships, and the comfort of being close to loved ones.

They made the trip to Canada as required by the PR process, but their decision was clear—they would not be relocating, at least not for now. The three-year window to make a definitive choice loomed ahead, but for them, the pull of home seemed far stronger than the allure of a foreign land.

As a parent, watching these milestones unfold in my children's lives has been both humbling and enlightening. Their journeys have been uniquely their own, shaped by their aspirations, circumstances, and the values instilled in them. Rohan's leap of faith to pursue opportunities in the U.S. was a testament to his courage and drive. Nidhi's choice to prioritize family, even as she held the key to a new life in Canada, spoke volumes about her sense of responsibility and love.

I often reflect on the foundation that binds us together as a family. While ambition and growth are celebrated, it is our shared values—love, respect, and the unwavering support for one another—that truly define us. I see these values reflected in my children's actions, in their decisions, and in the way they navigate the complexities of life.

In a world that often prioritizes individual success over collective well-being, I am proud of how Rohan and Nidhi have embraced both. Their choices, though different, stem from a common thread—the deep-rooted belief that family is not just a part of life, it is the heart of it.

The future remains unwritten. Whether Nidhi and Anish eventually settle in Canada or continue to build their lives here, only time will tell. For now, they are content, living in the present and cherishing the bonds that keep us close.

As for me, I carry the memories of these moments as precious reminders of what truly matters. Seeing my children grow, make their own choices, and stay grounded in their values fills me with gratitude. It is a legacy of love and strength, one that I hope they will carry forward in their own families someday.

And so, as I sit and reflect on this journey, I am reminded once again that life is not just about the destinations we reach but about the paths we choose, the people we walk with, and the values we uphold along the way.

CHAPTER 15

Finding My Purpose - Awakening the Coach Within

Pillars of Strength – Lessons That Shaped a Coach

There comes a time when, even the most deeply anchored roots begin to feel restless—not to flee the soil that holds them, but to seek the space to grow. After years of grounding myself in performance, outcomes, and expectations, I felt a quiet shift—an almost imperceptible stirring within. It wasn't a break, but a bending toward something new. A call to evolve, to extend into a different branch of my becoming, without letting go of what had come before. Coaching was that call—an answer to the silent question I had long set aside: What if your true impact lies not in leading from the front, but in helping others rise?

The hardest part of being a leader isn't the long hours, high-pressure decisions, or the endless pursuit of results. It's the moments when your role requires you to change the trajectory of someone else's life, sometimes against their will. Employee restructuring exercises are among the most soul-crushing tasks I've had to execute, and the emotional toll they took on me reshaped not only my leadership but also my understanding of humanity.

Each decision carried an unimaginable weight. A name on the list wasn't just a role to be eliminated but a livelihood, a family, a dream. And as much as I tried to approach these decisions with objectivity and professionalism, I couldn't shut off the human side of me. These were people I worked with daily—friends, colleagues, confidants—and I knew their stories, their struggles. It wasn't just a professional responsibility; it was personal.

What made it harder was the aftermath. Once the decisions were made, the late-night calls began. People were crying for answers, seeking clarity, or simply venting their frustrations. Some were inconsolable, breaking down over the phone, their pain palpable. As a leader, I felt obligated to be their anchor, to absorb their emotions, and to offer them reassurance even when I had none to give.

But what happens when the anchor starts to sink? Those conversations lingered in my mind long after the calls ended. I would lie awake at night, replaying their words, imagining their faces. Sleep became a luxury I couldn't afford. The emotional strain seeped into my health. I was perpetually exhausted, my body carrying the burden of my mind's turmoil. It wasn't long before I realized I couldn't continue like this.

Finding My Pillars of Strength

During this turbulent time, I was fortunate to have a few incredible people who became my pillars of strength. Each of them, in their unique way, taught me lessons that not only helped me navigate these challenges but also shaped the coach I would later become.

Dheeraj – Leadership with Heart

Dheeraj was a mentor, a sounding board, and, most importantly, a friend who reminded me that even leaders need support. He helped me understand that leadership was about finding the balance between caring for myself and others. He urged me to prioritize my health, emphasizing that I couldn't pour from an empty cup.

Under his guidance, I began taking small steps toward self-care—long walks, mindful eating, and learning to let go of what I couldn't control. Dheeraj's wisdom helped me see leadership not as a solitary burden but as a shared journey. His advice became a cornerstone of my coaching philosophy: to help others lead with compassion, not at the cost of their well-being.

Praveen Chandna – Meditation and Visualization

Praveen introduced me to the transformative power of meditation and visualization. At a time when my mind was a whirlwind of guilt, doubt, and worry, his guidance brought calm and clarity.

Through meditation, I learned to silence the noise in my head and find moments of peace amid chaos. Visualization, on the other hand, helped me reframe my fears and imagine positive outcomes. Praveen's teachings became a daily ritual for me, one that I carry forward to this day. These tools not only healed me but also became a valuable resource I now share with my coaching clients.

Ravi Bajaj – Journaling and Financial Clarity

Ravi was the pragmatist I needed in my life. He taught me the power of journaling—a simple yet profound practice that allowed me to organize my thoughts, process my emotions, and find clarity in the fog. Writing down my fears and feelings became a therapeutic outlet, one that helped me confront my inner turmoil head-on.

Ravi also introduced me to the concept of worst-case scenario planning. By putting my fears on paper and imagining the worst possible outcomes, I found a surprising sense of control and acceptance. His financial guidance was another layer of his wisdom, teaching me the importance of prudence and planning in times of uncertainty.

Maya – The Spiritual Connection

When I was struggling to find meaning amid the chaos, Urmila connected me with Maya, a spiritual guru who added a new dimension to my journey of recovery. Maya's approach was deeply rooted in introspection and spiritual alignment, helping me heal from within.

Through her, I learned to let go of guilt, embrace vulnerability, and trust the process of life. It was a spiritual awakening that added depth to my perspective, not just as a leader but as a human being.

Anju – My Anchor, Always

Through it all, my wife Anju was my unwavering source of strength. She saw me at my lowest—emotionally drained, physically exhausted, and mentally broken—and never once wavered. Her quiet resilience, her understanding, and her constant encouragement reminded me that I wasn't alone.

Anju didn't just support me; she held me together. Her strength gave me the courage to face each day and the wisdom to see that leadership is as much about relationships as it is about decisions.

Lessons That Shaped a Coach

These individuals didn't just help me through a difficult time—they gave me the tools and perspective that became the foundation of my coaching philosophy. Here's what I learned:

Leadership Is a Shared Journey: Dheeraj taught me the importance of seeking and offering support. No leader can succeed in isolation.

The Power of Practices: Meditation, journaling, and scenario planning became invaluable tools for managing stress and finding clarity.

Self-Care Is Non-Negotiable: You can't lead others effectively if you're running on empty.

Empathy Transforms Leadership: Every decision must balance logic with compassion.

Healing Through Connection: Whether it's through spiritual alignment or the strength of relationships, healing is a collaborative process.

Becoming a Coach

Looking back, these experiences were the crucible that forged me into the coach I am today. They taught me that leadership is more than achieving goals; it's about navigating the human side of challenges with grace and empathy.

When I sit with a client now—whether it's a corporate leader grappling with difficult decisions or an individual seeking clarity in life—I draw on these lessons. I share my journey, not to impress but to inspire, showing them that even in the darkest times, there is a path forward.

The people who stood by me during those years gave me more than just support; they gave me the blueprint for transformation. And for that, I am forever grateful.

The decision to establish my own coaching practice was a natural progression for me, but also a leap of faith. After decades of working in the corporate world, honing leadership skills, and engaging with people from diverse cultures and backgrounds, I had come to realize that my true calling lay in helping others navigate their professional lives. I had always been someone who believed in the power of transformation, and coaching seemed like the perfect platform to guide others toward unlocking their potential.

The journey began with a single, bold thought: "I want to make a meaningful difference." Having worked in leadership roles, I had gained substantial experience, yet it felt like there was more to life than just climbing the corporate ladder. I had always enjoyed mentoring colleagues, offering advice, and providing guidance, but making this transition into coaching was a huge decision. The prospect of moving from the comfort of a secure job to building something from scratch was daunting, to say the least.

From Banker to Coach: A Journey of Unlearning, Awakening, and Transformation

In my thirty years as a banker, I had become accustomed to the high-stakes world of finance—suits that fit too snugly, emails marked "urgent" that were rarely so, and the daily juggling act of managing teams that ranged from fresh-faced recruits to seasoned executives. It was a career that tested my patience, sharpened my instincts, and gave me a front-row seat to the power of transformation. But the irony was not lost on me:

even as I orchestrated transformations in organizations, I had neglected my own.

However, the transition from banker to coach was not a cake walk. It began, as these things often do, with a sense of disquiet I couldn't quite articulate. I realized I didn't have an answer. For decades, I had introduced myself as a banker, as if my profession were my entire identity. That moment hit me like a cold splash of water. It wasn't just an existential question; it was a challenge.

The decision to pursue coaching felt like jumping off a cliff without knowing how deep the water was. My first hurdle? The dreaded "imposter syndrome." Despite my years of experience mentoring individuals and leading diverse teams, stepping into the world of professional coaching felt like starting from scratch.

I took the first steps by enrolling for coaching certifications, studying various methodologies like NLP, CBT, Mindfulness and Applied Psychology, and immersing myself in the philosophy of human potential. But academic preparation could only take me so far. The true test lay in stepping into the market and convincing others of the value I could offer. My professional network was robust, but marketing myself as a coach was an entirely new arena. I was no longer the trusted executive. Now I was a coach who had to establish my credibility from the ground up.

I enrolled in a coaching program, only to discover that my corporate persona—confident, authoritative, and solution-oriented—was my greatest liability. Coaching, I learned, wasn't about having all the answers; it was about asking the right questions.

One particular session still makes me laugh. We were practicing active listening, and my cohort began sharing a deeply personal story. I couldn't resist the urge to jump in with advice, brimming with solutions before they had even finished speaking. Our mentor stopped me mid-sentence and said, "Anil, you're not here to fix their life. You're here to hold space for their discovery."

I remember muttering something about being a "problem solver by nature," to which she quipped, "Well, nature's wrong this time."

The Humbling Phase: Unlearning And Relearning

Unlearning was perhaps the hardest part of my journey. In the corporate world, I thrived on efficiency. Meetings were battles of wit, and there was an unspoken competition to see who could talk the most and say the least. Coaching, on the other hand, demanded silence, patience, and an almost meditative focus on the other person.

There were moments when I felt like a complete fraud. I remember one client, a highly ambitious entrepreneur, who came to me seeking clarity. Halfway through our session, she asked, "So, what do you think I should do?" My instinct was to launch into a SWOT analysis. Instead, I asked, "What do you think you want to do?"

Her silence stretched for what felt like an eternity. It was uncomfortable—for both of us. But in that silence, something shifted. They began to articulate their fears, hopes, and dreams in a way they never had before, and I realized that my value as a coach was in creating the ideal conditions for their own breakthroughs.

Introspection: The Mirror I Couldn't Avoid

As I coached others, I also began to coach myself. Coaching is, at its core, a deeply introspective process. You can't guide someone through their maze if you haven't navigated your own. I started to confront parts of myself I had ignored for decades—my fear of failure, my need for control, and my tendency to equate productivity with self-worth.

One particular incident comes to mind. During a mindfulness workshop, the facilitator asked us to write a letter to our younger selves. I pictured myself at twenty, fresh out of the Indian Military Academy, brimming with ambition and naivety. In my letter, I wrote: "Dear Anil, it's okay not to have all the answers. Life isn't a battlefield; it's a dance. Learn to move with the rhythm."

That exercise was a revelation. For the first time, I saw my life not as a linear climb but as a series of cycles—growth, stagnation, reinvention.

Of course, my journey wasn't without its comedic moments. During one of my early coaching sessions, I accidentally muted myself on Zoom and spent five minutes delivering what I thought was a profound monologue. My client, a millennial with a wicked sense of humor, waited patiently before saying, "That's a solid TED Talk, but can you unmute so I can hear it?"

Then there was the time I tried to use an NLP technique involving visualization. I asked my client to imagine a peaceful scene. They described a beach, complete with seagulls and crashing waves. When I asked them to picture their ideal self-walking on that beach, they said, "My ideal self would be in the Maldives, not on this zoom call."

These moments reminded me not to take myself too seriously. They served as a quiet reminder that effective coaching is rooted in authenticity, not perfection.

Discovering My Purpose

As I gained confidence, I began to see coaching not just as a profession but as a calling. It was humbling to witness people transform, not because of anything I said or did, but because they finally allowed themselves to be seen and heard.

One of my most rewarding experiences was coaching a middle manager on the verge of quitting their job. They felt stuck, unappreciated, and directionless. Over several sessions, they began to recognize their own patterns of self-sabotage. By the end of our engagement, they had not only stayed in their role but had also been promoted. They later told me, "You didn't just help me with my career; you helped me find myself."

Moments like these reaffirmed my decision to leave banking. In the corporate world, success was measured in numbers—revenue, profit margins, market share. In coaching, success was far more personal. It was in the quiet moments of clarity, the breakthroughs that seemed small, were, in fact, monumental.

The Fulfillment of Helping Others Navigate Their Professional Lives

As the weeks turned into months, and my client base began to grow, the initial fears of self-doubt and uncertainty faded. Coaching provided an unparalleled sense of fulfillment, one that I had never experienced in my corporate roles. It wasn't about financial success or career advancement anymore; it was about making a real, tangible difference in the lives of others. There's something incredibly rewarding about helping someone see their own potential when they previously couldn't. It's like guiding someone through a fog, only to see them emerge with a newfound clarity and purpose.

One of the most profound aspects of coaching was watching my clients transform in real time. The growth wasn't just limited to their careers—it extended to their personal lives, their sense of self-worth, and their ability to navigate the world with confidence. Each success story was a victory not just for the client but for me as well. Knowing that I had played a role in helping someone unlock their potential was the most fulfilling aspect of my new career.

I also found that coaching provided a unique opportunity to work with people from all walks of life. The diversity of my clients was immense: executives looking to take the next step in their careers, professionals navigating the tricky waters of work-life balance, individuals recovering from setbacks, and those struggling with career direction. Each session was different, but each was rooted in one common theme: personal growth. It wasn't always easy, and it wasn't always linear, but the transformation was always worth the effort.

One of the more humbling aspects of my coaching practice was how people would trust me with their most vulnerable moments—moments of self-doubt, uncertainty, and personal struggle. The sense of responsibility was immense, but so was the privilege. To be invited into someone's life and trusted with their dreams and challenges was something I never took lightly. This trust was the foundation upon which my coaching practice grew, and over time, it evolved into a deeper understanding of the true power of coaching, not just as a career, but as a calling.

A New Chapter

Today, as a professional coach, I feel a sense of fulfillment I never experienced in banking. My days are no longer consumed by spreadsheets and strategy meetings. Instead, they are filled with conversations that matter—conversations that change lives.

And while my journey from banker to coach wasn't smooth or straightforward, it was exactly what I needed. It taught me that success isn't about climbing the corporate ladder; it's about helping others find the courage to climb their own.

So, if you're reading this and wondering whether it's time to reinvent yourself, my advice is simple: Take the leap. Yes, you'll stumble, and yes, you'll doubt yourself. But in the end, you'll discover parts of yourself you never knew existed. And that, my friend, is worth everything.

CHAPTER 16

The Final Blueprint: Thriving in Life and Leadership

As I reflect on the trajectory of my life, the lessons I've learned, the challenges I've faced, and the growth I've undergone, it becomes clear to me that success in life and leadership is not a matter of mere chance or circumstance; it is the result of intentional decisions, continuous learning, and building meaningful relationships. Over the years, I have navigated some of the most demanding environments, from the structured discipline of the Indian Military Academy (IMA) to the fast-paced world of international banking, and finally, to my current role as a coach and mentor. Each phase of my life has imparted lessons that have been crucial to not only achieving success but also living a fulfilling life.

In this chronicle, I seek to distill the key lessons that have shaped my journey—lessons that I believe will resonate with future leaders, entrepreneurs, and professionals. These are insights that have helped me thrive despite adversity and that continue to guide me as I strive to make an impact, both personally and professionally.

1. The Power of Self-Awareness and Self-Discipline

The journey to becoming a successful leader or entrepreneur begins with one fundamental truth: self-awareness. The ability to understand your own emotions, strengths, weaknesses, and the impact you have on others is the cornerstone of effective leadership. My time at IMA was pivotal in developing this self-awareness. When I first joined, I was confronted with the rigorous demands of military life, and I quickly realized that my previous sense of self wasn't enough to survive, let alone excel, in such an environment. The harsh realities of army life forced me to look inward and recognize my own vulnerabilities. I had to acknowledge my weaknesses, manage my emotions under stress, and embrace discipline.

The discipline I learned during those early years shaped how I approached every subsequent challenge. It wasn't just about performing tasks on time or meeting deadlines—it was about maintaining a high level of commitment to every decision I made, regardless of external pressures. Whether I was leading a multinational team or navigating a personal crisis, self-discipline became the anchor that kept me grounded. I learned that success isn't just about achieving goals; it's about staying committed to your values, regardless of the obstacles that arise.

For future leaders and entrepreneurs, my advice is simple: Develop a deep sense of self-awareness and commit to self-discipline. Know your strengths and weaknesses, and never stop improving. Leadership begins with knowing who you are and making decisions aligned with your core principles. This internal clarity will guide you in the most challenging times.

2. Resilience: The Key to Overcoming Adversity

Resilience is a trait that I have come to value more than anything else. Throughout my life, I've faced numerous setbacks, from leaving the army to navigating complex corporate dynamics to dealing with personal losses. Each of these challenges could have easily led to a sense of defeat, but resilience, both emotional and mental, has been the key to bouncing back and moving forward. The ability to face adversity, learn from it, and emerge stronger is what defines a true leader.

One of the most defining moments of resilience in my career came when I was in Botswana. After spending years in the corporate world, I was sent to manage the bank in a completely unfamiliar environment. The country, culture, business landscape, and internal work dynamics were all new to me, and the challenges seemed insurmountable. But rather than retreating or resigning myself to failure, I chose to lean into the discomfort. I engaged deeply with local teams, learned the nuances of their culture, and listened to their insights. Over time, I gained their trust, and together we achieved success. This experience taught me that resilience is not about being impervious to hardship, but about staying open to learning and staying steadfast in the face of adversity.

Another pivotal lesson in resilience came during my time at HSBC. A sudden restructuring within the organization left many employees uncertain about their future. It would have been easy to focus solely on the operational and business side of the process, but I understood that the emotional well-being of the employees was just as important. By fostering open communication and providing support, I helped the team navigate the changes. Resilience, I realized, wasn't just about personal strength—it was about lifting others up during difficult times as well.

For those starting out in their careers or embarking on entrepreneurial ventures, my advice is clear: Embrace resilience as a core value. Understand that setbacks are a natural part of the journey. The key is to not let these obstacles define you but to let them refine you. Every failure is an opportunity to learn, grow, and become better.

3. The Importance of Empathy and Emotional Intelligence

Empathy and emotional intelligence are two of the most powerful tools a leader can possess. It's easy to assume that leadership is all about making decisions and driving outcomes, but true leadership is grounded in the ability to connect with others, understand their perspectives, and respond with compassion.

I learned the importance of empathy during my time in Botswana. There were many moments where misunderstandings arose due to cultural differences, and in those moments, my ability to empathize and understand the underlying emotions was critical.

Empathy is not just about understanding others' emotions—it's about responding with care and consideration. It's about being present and actively engaging with the needs and challenges of those around you. This ability to connect on a human level has been key to building strong relationships, both in business and in my personal life.

For future leaders, entrepreneurs, and professionals, I would advise: Never underestimate the power of empathy. Cultivate emotional intelligence by learning to recognize your own emotions and those of others. In business, as in life, the ability to navigate relationships with understanding and respect is what sets great leaders apart.

4. The Importance of Strong Relationships

As I look back on my career and personal life, one of the greatest lessons I've learned is the importance of building and nurturing strong relationships. No success is achieved in isolation, and no leader thrives without the support of others. Throughout my career, I've been fortunate to build lasting relationships with colleagues, mentors, and clients who have helped me grow. It is through these relationships that I have learned the most about leadership, resilience, and personal growth.

One of the most impactful relationships in my life was with my mentor, who guided me through many of the toughest decisions in my career. His advice, often laced with wisdom and humor, helped me see the bigger picture during times of crisis. But equally important were the relationships I built with my teams and colleagues. It was through these relationships that I learned how to lead with authenticity, how to listen with empathy, and how to inspire others to achieve their best.

The importance of maintaining strong relationships extends to family and friends as well. While professional success is important, it is the support and love of family that provides the foundation for true fulfillment. In my own life, my family has been my pillar of strength. During times of personal loss, such as the death of my parents, it was their steadfast support that helped me through the toughest of times.

For those embarking on their own journeys, I would advise: Never underestimate the value of relationships. Invest time in building meaningful connections, whether with your team, colleagues, mentors, or loved ones. These relationships will be your greatest source of strength and wisdom throughout your life.

5. The Pursuit of Continual Growth

Success is not a destination—it's a journey. And the key to thriving in both life and leadership is the commitment to continual growth. No matter how successful you become or how high you rise, there is always more to learn, more to improve, and more to give.

My journey has been one of constant evolution. From my time in the military academy to my roles in multinational corporations to becoming a coach and mentor, I have consistently sought opportunities for growth—whether through further education, self-reflection, or engaging with new challenges. The world around us is constantly changing, and the ability to adapt and evolve is what enables us to stay relevant and impactful.

One of the most important aspects of continual growth is being open to feedback. In my career, I've always welcomed constructive criticism as an opportunity to improve. This openness to learning, even from mistakes or failures, is what has allowed me to keep progressing. Leadership, like life, is a journey of constant development, and the willingness to embrace change is essential for anyone striving for success.

For those seeking to build a successful and fulfilling life, I would say: Commit to lifelong learning. Seek feedback, embrace new challenges, and always look for ways to improve yourself. Growth is the foundation upon which all success is built.

As I draw the final blueprint of my journey, the key lessons are clear: self-awareness, resilience, empathy, strong relationships, and the pursuit of continual growth. These are the pillars that have supported me throughout my life, guiding me through both personal and professional challenges.

To the next generation of leaders, entrepreneurs, and professionals, I offer this advice: Build a foundation of self-awareness and discipline. Embrace resilience as a natural part of the journey. Lead with empathy and emotional intelligence, and always nurture the relationships that matter most. Finally, commit to continual growth. Success is not a destination but a lifelong pursuit.

In the end, the true measure of success lies not in accolades or achievements, but in the impact, we have on others and the legacy we leave behind. It's about thriving in life, not just surviving, and leaving a blueprint for others to follow—one that is grounded in authenticity, growth, and connection.

EPILOGUE

The Compass of a Well-Lived Life

As I stand at the crossroads of reflection and future possibilities, I cannot help but marvel at the journey that has brought me to this point. From the early days as an air force kid, growing up in an environment that instilled discipline and a sense of duty, to my experiences navigating the corporate world, and later transitioning into a coach and mentor, my path has been shaped by a diverse tapestry of experiences, challenges, and triumphs. Each chapter of my life has played a crucial role in molding the person I am today—both the leader I've become and the individual I strive to be.

Looking back, I see how my upbringing—living in various places across India and encountering a multitude of cultures and perspectives—formed the bedrock of my leadership style. The values of hard work, integrity, and respect for others that my parents instilled in me were essential in shaping my character. As I grew older and my career took me across different countries and industries, I realized that the principles I learned early on were universal—they could be applied in every context, whether I was in the Indian Military Academy, working in international banks, or dealing with clients and colleagues from all walks of life.

The challenges I faced along the way were equally formative. It's not just about bouncing back from setbacks; it's about staying committed to your purpose and embracing the discomfort of change and growth.

Through it all, I learned that leadership is not about the myth of having the highest titles or the most accolades. It's about the ability to inspire, guide, and uplift others. I learned that true leadership is rooted in empathy, understanding, and emotional intelligence. The leaders who left the greatest impact on me were not those who demanded results, but those who listened, who cared, and who understood the human side of business and life. This lesson in leadership has been a cornerstone of my career, and I have tried to pass it on to those I mentor and coach today.

But leadership extends beyond the workplace. It stretches into our personal lives, where relationships are the true measure of success. The support I've received from my family, my mentors, and my colleagues has been invaluable. I've learned that no one achieves success in isolation. We thrive when we lift others up, when we surround ourselves with people who challenge us, support us, and help us grow.

As I reflect on these experiences, I am reminded of the importance of resilience and adaptability. Life is filled with challenges—some expected, others completely unforeseen. The key is not to shy away from these challenges but to face them head-on, with a mindset of growth and learning. It's easy to get caught in the cycle of fear and self-doubt, especially in times of crisis. But it's through adversity that we discover our true strength.

For anyone reading this who may be navigating their own challenges, my advice is simple: Don't give up. Stay true to your values, keep moving forward, and remember that setbacks are not failures—they are opportunities for growth. Leadership, whether in business, life, or personal development, is a lifelong journey. It's about continuously evolving, learning, and, most importantly, staying resilient in the face of adversity.

Now, as I stand on the precipice of this chapter of my life, the road that stretches ahead seems as exhilarating as it is uncertain. My journey, with its twists and turns, has not followed a single, linear path. It has been marked by moments of decision, reflection, and action — some deliberate, others borne out of necessity. But every experience has contributed to the person I am today, and now, as I look to the future, I find myself driven by a sense of anticipation and purpose that is stronger than ever before.

Life is not static, and neither is the meaning we find in it. As I now stand at this crossroads, I know that the road ahead is not just about looking back at what I've achieved but about continuing to chart a course for the person I am yet to become. The past has been a guide, but it is the future that is my compass.

The most important question I face is no longer "Who am I?" but "Who do I want to become?" As I grow further into my role as a coach, I see the potential to deepen my understanding of human behavior and leadership even further. The pursuit of wisdom and knowledge is a lifelong journey, and my learning will continue to be shaped by the people I meet, the experiences I gain, and the stories I am entrusted with.

In the years ahead, I hope to expand my coaching practice further, reaching new people and new audiences. I see my work as a way to help others find their own paths — paths that are not constrained by the limitations of the past, but instead are illuminated by the possibilities of the future.

I also see the potential for expanding my impact in ways that go beyond individual coaching. I have begun to think about ways to create larger platforms for learning and leadership, whether through books, seminars, online courses, or community initiatives. Moreover, I am eager to take more action, to invest in projects and initiatives that allow me to make a larger impact on the world.

One of the most exciting possibilities that lies ahead is the intersection of technology and coaching. In an era of rapid change, the ways in which we work, learn, and grow are evolving quickly. Coaching, once seen as a one-on-one, face-to-face interaction, is now being transformed by virtual platforms, apps, and AI-driven tools. While the human connection remains at the core of coaching, I am excited to explore the possibilities of using technology to reach more people, offer more resources, and create a scalable impact.

This shift presents both challenges and opportunities. As I embrace new technologies, I will also need to remain grounded in the principles that have always guided my work: authenticity, empathy, and the power of human connection. The future is a delicate balance between embracing the new and staying rooted in what has proven effective. But I am confident that with the right mindset, the possibilities for growth and transformation are endless.

Mentorship and Legacy

Another thing I most look forward to is the opportunity to mentor the next generation of leaders, coaches, and changemakers. My journey has been one of evolution, and I want to be able to pass on the lessons I have learned to those who will carry the torch forward.

In many ways, mentorship is an extension of the work I already do as a coach. It is about helping others see their own potential and guiding them as they take the next steps on their path. But mentorship, in the traditional sense, offers something deeper: it is about creating lasting connections that transcend the professional sphere. A mentor has the ability to impact someone's life in ways that are not just career-focused but also life-altering. I want to be that kind of mentor — one who helps people develop not just their skills, but their sense of self.

Looking at the future of leadership, I see a generation that is increasingly aware of the importance of purpose, of ethics, and of empathy in leadership. The leaders of tomorrow are not just seeking financial success; they are driven by a desire to make a meaningful impact. As someone who has experienced the full arc of leadership, from the army to the corporate world to coaching, I feel a deep sense of responsibility to help cultivate these new leaders.

The mentorship I give today will create the legacy I leave for tomorrow. And it is that legacy, not just of personal success but of collective growth and transformation, that is one of the greatest sources of fulfillment I can imagine.

Not Settling but Setting Forth

As I write this, I am filled with a calm kind of wonder—a quiet excitement that hums beneath the surface. There is still much to unfold, and the road ahead stretches wide with possibility. In many ways, the most vital, expansive chapter of my life still awaits.

The world spins faster each day, shifting beneath our feet. And yet, amidst the swirl of change, some truths remain: our need for connection, for growth, for a sense of purpose. These are my north stars—the quiet constants that steady me, that keep me leaning into what's next.

Some roots dig deeper. Others reach forward. Mine have always moved—restless, seeking, quietly unsettled. That longing, that pulse of becoming, has shaped my journey—and now shapes the work I do with others.

So let your roots never harden in place. Let them twist and stretch beneath you—turning, reaching, reshaping the ground as they go. Let them grow into paths, winding and unseen, and let them climb too—rising through the dark toward light, like trees learning how to touch the sky.

If your roots feel unsettled lately, know this: you are not lost. You are awakening. You are not broken. You are becoming. The path ahead may be unfamiliar, but it holds promise. Listen to the quiet tug within—the one that whispers, you are ready for more.

The best is still becoming. And so are you.

THE DEEPEST ROOT

For a lifetime chronicled by **Restless Roots,** the quietest, most sacred place to finally land was always ahead.

That landing arrived on 25Sep2025, not as a destination, but as the tiny, perfect hand of **Naomika,** my daughter's daughter. Her name, a grace note whispered into the rushing stream of time, is the melody of renewal. All the searching woven into these chapters—the yearning, the movement—was merely the long road leading to this moment of profound stillness.

In her eyes, the world begins again. She is the bloom upon the branch, the legacy taking its first breath, and the sweetest evidence that the greatest adventures always lead us home.

Welcome, little one. The roots are restless no more.

NOTES